THE OAKWOOD PRESS  X50

SOUTHERN RAILWAY PASSENGER VANS

by
David Gould

THE OAKWOOD PRESS

© Oakwood Press 1992

ISBN 0 85361 428 8

Typeset by Gem Publishing Company, Brightwell, Wallingford, Oxfordshire.
Printed by Alpha Print (Oxon) Ltd, Witney, Oxon.

A milk train passing Woking in the 1930s. Working from the engine we see a PL van,
a GBL van, a fixed milk tank, a former SE&C 6-wheeled brake van, two 6-wheeled
trucks carrying United Dairies mobile tankk trailers, and a PL van bringing up the rear.

F. Foote

Published by
The OAKWOOD PRESS
P.O.Box 122, Headington, Oxford.

Contents

Note:
All the drawings have been reproduced to the largest size to fit the page and not to any scale. Each drawing has measurements included to allow for re-scaling for modelling use.

Acknowledgements

Most of the information herein has been obtained from the same sources as that contained in *Maunsell's SR Steam Carriage Stock*, published by The Oakwood Press in 1990. In addition, I am indebted to all the following for supplying me with various notes:

Tom Burnham – information about milk tanks taken from *The Engineer* (15.7.32 and 17.6.32) and *Railway Gazette* (9.12.27, 9.10.31 and 2.6.33).

Richard Casserley – withdrawal dates of vans during the 1960s and 1970s.

Denis Cullum – clarified a number of obscure points.

R.W. Kidner – information on milk trains working in the 1930s taken from *Over the Points*, September 1931.

Mike King – a vast amount of information about SR vans and clarification of details of SECR vans. In particular I am most grateful to Mike for allowing his excellent 4 mm scale drawings of SR vans to be reproduced in this book.

May 1992   *D. Gould*
                                                                   East Grinstead

Introduction

Southern Railway passenger vans had a style all their own. Although the other British railways, between the Wars, usually modelled their brake and luggage vans on the style of their coaches, most of which at this time were steel-clad on timber body-framing, the Southern remained faithful to timber-planked bodywork for its vans. Consequently its passenger vans bore a marked family likeness to its goods vans, even to the characteristic low elliptical roof, although the bodies were much longer and sometimes on bogies. Only the mail-sorting carriages, built to the requirements of the General Post Office, followed the current SR coaching stock style.

The Southern built 4-wheeled and bogie versions of brake vans, luggage vans and covered carriage trucks. Unlike the London, Midland & Scottish and the London & North Eastern Railways, the Southern never built any 6-wheeled vans, as it preferred long-wheelbase 4-wheelers (21 ft). Only the bogie luggage vans were graced with corridor connections, not counting the off-centre gangways fitted to the post office vans. A curious distinction between brake vans and luggage-only vans was that the former always had droplights in the doors but no windows on the bodyside, while the latter always had fixed lights in the bodyside but no droplights in any doors. Brake vans always had a centrally placed guard's compartment, equipped with electric light and steam heater; luggage vans were generally empty shells (only the bogie vans were electrically lit) and steam-piped only.

Also included in this survey are milk tanks because, although they physically resembled wagons, they were in reality passenger-rated vehicles, technically open carriage trucks on which were mounted either fixed or mobile tanks. All were fully fitted with vacuum brakes and were through-piped for steam heating.

The fact that Southern vans were numbered in a separate series meant that several van numbers duplicated coach numbers. Only the London & South Western had numbered all its coaching stock vehicles in one series, but at Grouping the SR's rolling stock clerks decided to follow the South Eastern & Chatham system of having passenger coaches in one series (which for the Southern ran from 1 to 10,000) and the vans in another (running from 1 to 4960). Originally, guard's vans started at 1, luggage vans at 1251, horse boxes at 2501, cattle vans at 3651, open carriage trucks at 3901, covered carriage trucks at 4501 and post office vans at 4901. As with the coaching stock list, pre-Grouping vans were renumbered in the order LSW, SEC and London, Brighton & South Coast, with gaps to allow for new construction. When these were filled, new vehicles began to take the numbers of withdrawn stock.

Construction of SR passenger vans began in 1928, five years into Grouping, and was continuous up to 1944. A batch then came in 1947, the last year of the Southern's existence, but the design was clearly too good then to die with the Southern and British Railways built hundreds more in 1950, 1951 and as late as 1955. Southern numbers were given an 'S' prefix from 1948, but a year later received an 'S' suffix in addition. The prefix indicated the operating Region and the suffix the pre-Nationalisation Company. The Isle of Wight, always a law unto itself, did not follow this system and coaching stock vehicles there carried only the prefix and never a suffix letter. The seven Southern-built vans that had been shipped across the Solent in 1950 were the only post-Grouping stock in the Island! In the mid-1970s someone decided that the 'S' suffix was superfluous and it was deleted in all future repaints, even though there was a risk of confusion with BR standard vehicles bearing the same number, or even with other pre-Nationalisation van stock, of which there was still a fair number.

The variety of traffic carried in passenger vans until the 1960s was astounding, in retrospect, though doubtless taken for granted at the time. Taking the summer of 1955 as an example, we find the following commodities being conveyed in passenger vans on the London East District:

Milk in churns: Wallens Dairies and the Co-operative Wholesale Society's churns were sent from Victoria to Shorncliffe, Gillingham, Tunbridge Wells West, Dover Priory, Ashford, Faversham, Folkestone, Margate and Sitting-bourne by night parcels trains.

Lyons' Cakes: a daily van of cakes ran from Margate to Maidstone West.

Lyons' Teashop traffic in trays: from Kensington via Clapham Junction to London Bridge or Holborn, thence Canterbury, Chatham, Maidstone, Margate and Ramsgate. Delivery to these stations was expected not later than 7.0 am each morning.

Mushrooms from Ashford and Headcorn: forwarded to Charing Cross every Sunday, thence by road to Euston and rail to Manchester.

Oysters from Whitstable: carried on Sundays in a van running in the 10.40 am parcels train from Ramsgate to Holborn, detached at Blackfriars.

Also conveyed were mails and parcels, newspapers, racing pigeons, fish and fruit. It must be remembered that in those days British Railways provided a public service, which may or may not have lost money; but when BR decided it was a 'business' it felt free to discontinue any traffic that it deemed unprofitable and nowadays, at least in the South, not a single one of the commodities mentioned above is conveyed. No doubt BR rubbed its hands in glee – it had also saved itself the bother of building any replacement vans when the Southern vehicles became due for withdrawal!

However, at least until the mid-1970s, there was still a very large amount of mails and parcels being carried and there were several overnight van trains. Every night fast newspaper trains left Victoria and Waterloo and it was unthinkable that they should ever be discontinued; but it happened, in 1988, although by then all Southern vans had been withdrawn. Until the early 1970s extra parcels trains ran during the hectic pre-Christmas rush, and London Bridge Low Level was given over entirely to accommodating mail trains. From 1963 there was a shortage of spare vans and the practice began of loading mailbags into electric multiple units, which ran as parcels trains between morning and evening peak duties.

When I began taking a serious interest in Southern coaches, in 1961, vans did not attract much attention. They all looked very similar, they were very common and they didn't run as part of set trains. Some numbers were taken, in a haphazard way: in 1961 I saw bogie vans Nos. 241 at Tonbridge, 228 at Redhill and 367 at Oxted. There was an interesting operation every morning at Oxted. A bogie brake van would come down on the rear of the 8.01 am from London Bridge to Tunbridge Wells and be left standing in the down platform. The push-and-pull train standing in the down bay platform would move out after the 8.01 had left and then set back into the main platform to pick up the van, which it then took to Tunbridge Wells via Ashurst at 9.04 am. Van No. 364 was recorded on this working in March 1962. Another train conveying a bogie brake van was the 10.35 am Tonbridge to Redhill; on 12th April, 1962 I noted No. 275 on this train as it entered Redhill. What I didn't know was that the van was on the same diagram as the Oxted one noted above! The working started with the 3.27 am van train from London Bridge as far as Three Bridges, from where it was sent by freight train to Forest Row and another freight to East Grinstead. Next day it was on the 6.34 am to London Bridge, 8.01 am London Bridge to Oxted, 9.04 am thence to Tunbridge Wells West and 9.40 am van train to Tonbridge. On arrival at Redhill it was attached to the 5.32 pm van train from Brighton to London Bridge.

Although large numbers of withdrawn vans had their lives extended by being used as departmental service vehicles, most of them had been condemned by 1990. It is to the private railways that one must turn in order to see SR vans, of which a surprisingly large number have been preserved. In addition, their underframes have often been found useful in giving life once again to really ancient carriage bodies which had stood around as henhouses and suchlike for the past 60 years.

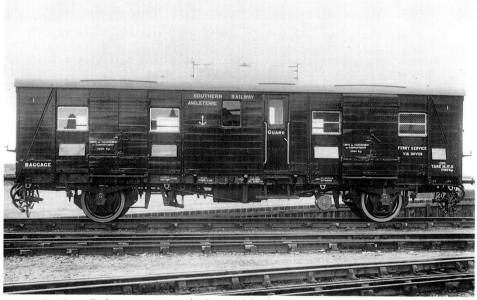

Southern Railway van No. 1, built at Ashford in June 1936 for the 'Night Ferry' service. Blue livery, lettering in English and French, vacuum and air brakes fitted.
Author's Collection

Chapter One
4-wheeled Guard's Vans (Night Ferry)

In March 1934 three guard's vans were authorised to be built for use in a proposed train service working between London and Paris by way of a new train ferry from Dover to Dunkerke. The vans were completed at Ashford in June 1936 to Order No. 825 (Diagram 3091) and received the numbers 1 to 3. The Night Ferry service itself began on 14th October, 1936 (several months later than had been hoped), using specially-constructed Wagon-Lits sleeping cars.

Nos. 1–3 were dual-braked, steam-heated and electrically lit. They measured 36 ft over headstocks, 7 ft 10¼ in. over body width (8 ft 8¼ in. overall width) and were 11 ft 7 in. from rail to roof – which had a shallow ellipse, quite unlike the normal profile of SR vans. This was designed to accommodate a centrally-placed roof lookout to conform to French practice, and the top of this was 12 ft 8 in. from rail level. Guard's doors, which opened inwards, were opposite each other and inset 4½ inches from the bodyside. Two luggage compartments, each of which was 14 ft 1 in. long, flanked the centrally-placed guard's compartment and the battery boxes were accommodated in one of the luggage compartments as there was insufficient space below the floor. This area was filled with vacuum-brake cylinders and reservoir, Westinghouse brake cylinders and reservoir, and dynamo for lighting generation.

Safety chains were fitted to the headstocks and there were lugs on the solebars to secure the vans while on the ferry. A communication cord ran along the roof and was carried over the top of the lookout by rodding and cranks.

The vans were painted deep blue to match the colour of the sleeping cars and the yellow lettering was a mixture of French and English. 'Southern Railway Angleterre'; 'Baggage'; 'Limite de Chargement du Compartiment 5000 kgs'; 'Ferry Service via Dover'; and 'Tare 16,17,0, 17120 kgs' were distributed randomly over the bodyside.

Except during World War II, these vans ran daily in the Night Ferry until 1960, two in traffic (one on each train-set) and one spare. After 1948, lettering changes included 'British Railways Angleterre' and 'Tare 16–16–0, 17070 kgs'. In 1960 the vans were taken off Night Ferry duty and several modifications made. The Westinghouse brake equipment, the safety chains and the external communication cords were all removed and Nos. 1–3 were repainted in standard Southern Region green. Some years later the lighting was stripped and they became regarded as purely luggage vans, without guard.

No. 1 was withdrawn from service in March 1969; No. 2 in June 1969; and No. 3 in July 1974. Eventually all were broken up.

CHANNEL FERRY PASSENGER BRAKE VAN

NOS. 1 - 3.

DIAGRAM No. 3091

TARE 17 TONS

11'-7"

1'-10"

14'-1"

EMERGENCY BRAKE
GEAR RODDING

GUARD'S COMPT.

7'-2¾"

14'-1"

DYNAMO THIS
SIDE

AIR
RESERVOIR

23'-0"

36'-0"

V.C. CYLINDER
THIS SIDE ONLY

SOUTHERN RAILWAY
ANGLE BRAKE

SOUTHERN RAILWAY
ANGLE BRAKE

GUARD

WESTINGHOUSE BRAKE
CYLINDER THIS SIDE

NOTE:- GUARD'S DOOR IS INSET 4½" FROM BODYSIDE

13'-0" OVER BRAKE
RODDING

SAFETY
CHAINS

7'-10¾" OVER
BODY

8'-10½"
OVER HANDLES

DRAWN BY
M. S. KING

Ferry van No. 2 in use on a train at Dover Marine. Clearly visible is the roof observatory and the recessed door for the guard. *M.S. King*

Former ferry van No. 3 in later BR days, classified 'BY' and repainted green. This van, built at Ashford in June 1936, was withdrawn in July 1974. Here standing at London Bridge. *Author's Collection*

4-wheeled guard's van No. 716, built at Eastleigh in July 1938. Note planking style: alternating pairs of planks 6½ in. and 3½ in. wide; lozenge-shaped panels for chalking destinations and twin periscopes on the roof.

Courtesy National Railway Museum

Stove-fitted guard's van (as indicated by orange panels at top corners and on guard's door) No. 405, built at Ashford (*underframe*) and Eastleigh (*body*) in June 1937. Here seen at London Bridge. *M.S. King*

Chapter Two
4-wheeled Guard's Vans

As the Southern Railway had inherited a very large number of 6-wheeled passenger guard's vans from its constituent companies it did not at first need to build any new ones. When eventually a design was prepared it was for 4-wheeled rather than 6-wheeled vehicles: in fact it was a 'stretched' version of the standard 32 ft luggage vans (see later) with a body length of 36 ft and wheelbase of 23 ft.

A batch of 50 vans was ordered in March 1936 (Order No. A928) and built at Eastleigh with Ashford-built underframes in June and July 1937. Vehicle numbers were 400–49; Diagram No. 3092. Each van had a central guard's compartment with outward-opening doors at cross-corners, and it was flanked by two luggage compartments each 15 ft 5⁷⁄₁₆ in. long. Maximum width of the body was 8 ft 10⅞ in. and height from rail to roof was 12 ft (12 ft 8 in. to top of periscope). A periscope was a standard fitting for guard's vans on the Southern. On the bodyside, two sets of double doors, each with a droplight, gave access to the luggage compartments. The body had horizontal planking arranged in alternate pairs 3½ in. and 6½ in. wide – a curious arrangement favoured by the Southern for all van construction from 1938, and first introduced on these brake vans. Vacuum brakes, electric lighting and steam heating equipment were all fitted. Tare weight was 16 tons, carrying capacity 10 tons. Some of the new vans were used on both passenger and parcels trains on the 'Chatham' main line from summer, 1937.

One hundred more guard's vans were authorised in March 1937. The first 20 were built wholly at Ashford but the rest had Ashford-built underframes and Eastleigh-built bodies, identical to the 1937 batch. Nos. 651–70 were completed in August and September 1938, whilst the Eastleigh allocation, Nos. 671–750, was turned out between March and July 1938. All 100 were to Order No. A974.

Construction continued with 50 more vans, to Order No. A1030, being completed by Ashford (frames) and Eastleigh (bodies) between March and October 1939; these were Nos. 751–800. Finally, a batch of 50 was built with underframes by Lancing and bodies by Eastleigh (Order No. L1090) during 1940 and 1941, these being Nos. 931–80. There was thus a total of 250 4-wheeled guard's vans to Diagram 3092.

Southern Railway code for these brake vans was 'Van C'. From July 1938 a Van C was formed in the 1.30 am newspaper train from Waterloo to Plymouth, being loaded for Bulford. Later in 1938 Nos. 660 and 661 received roofboards and were stencilled on the solebars 'To work between Yeovil and Derby'. They were allocated to the following regular workings on weekdays:

	dep.		dep.
Yeovil	6.15 pm	Derby	3.50 am
Yeovil Jn.	6.35 pm	Templecombe	2.25 pm
Templecombe	8.12 pm	Yeovil Jn.	3.50 pm
Derby	–	Yeovil	–

The vans carried dairy products from Messrs Aplin & Barrett's depot at Yeovil until the contract was suddenly terminated in August 1939.

In 1941 many of the night trains from Waterloo were arranged to start their journeys from either Victoria or Surbiton, probably to avoid the worst of the London bombing at that time. The 1.30 am paper train started from Wimbledon at 1.40 am and included a Van C for Salisbury, going forward at 3.35 am for Yeovil. A Van C for Brockenhurst was included in the 3.15 am departure from Surbiton, and two vans were in the 5.04 am Wimbledon to Alton. By 1946 the now-retimed 1.25 am from Waterloo had a van for Bulford, the 4.25 am (Mondays excepted) had one for Chertsey via Ascot and Woking, the 1.05 am Clapham Junction to Stewarts Lane included a Van C for Folkestone Harbour, and the 3.0 am (MX) from Clapham Junction had a van for Woking.

A small batch of safe-fitted guard's vans was constructed in October 1941 to Order No. 1091. Nos. 10–14 had underframes built at Lancing and bodies at Eastleigh. Although similar in appearance to Diagram 3092, these 15-ton vans were distinguished by the vehicle number being painted in large white figures on a red panel. The safe extended the width of the van, with a small external door on each bodyside but no access from the guard's compartment. On each of these vans (Diagram No. 3094) the guard's compartment was 7 ft 3 in. long instead of 4 ft 6 in., which resulted in a smaller luggage compartment at one end, 12 ft 8⁷⁄₁₆ in. long. The other luggage compartment, which incorporated the safe, was 15 ft 5⁷⁄₁₆ in. as usual.

By 1941 twenty 4-wheel guard's vans had been fitted with stoves. Such a fitting was necessary if a van should find itself in a goods train, with no chance of any steam heat getting through from the locomotive because goods wagons had no through steam pipes. Even in parcels trains there was no guarantee that the engine crew would connect the steam-heating pipes to the train.

The vehicles involved were Nos. 400–19; these stove-fitted vans were distinguished by an orange panel painted on the body and were not allowed to be worked off the SR. Also by 1941, Nos. 400/1 had been fitted with side lamp irons for working in West of England fast freight services. These vans were rather more comfortable for the guard than the usual goods brake van!

Some vans were damaged during the War, but all were repaired and returned to traffic. On 8th September, 1940 a high-explosive bomb fell on Clapham Junction carriage sheds, causing much damage to stock, including Van C No. 753. Incendiaries falling on Portsmouth & Southsea on 4th May, 1941 burned two holes in the roof of No. 949 (recorded as the Nurse Cavell Van). No. 681 was reconstructed at Eastleigh in January 1942 after enemy action damage, and No. 712, which was damaged by enemy action in August 1944, afterwards received repairs.

After nationalisation of the Southern Railway on 1st January, 1948, green remained the standard livery for vans; but in 1949 it was decreed that 'crimson lake' be used for all further repaints. This so-called crimson was not the rich shade used by the old London, Midland & Scottish Railway but a carmine red, not unattractive: the same colour was used on non-corridor passenger coaches. Red was standard until July 1956. Probably all the guard's vans (coded BY under the standard BR system) were repainted 'crimson'; for example No. 689 received this colour at Lancing Works in July

Guard's van No. 442, built at Ashford and Eastleigh in June 1937, in use as a brake van on a passenger train at Horsted Keynes on the preserved Bluebell Railway, 7th September, 1986. *Author*

4-wheel guard's van No. 404 on the Bluebell Railway, showing battery boxes, channel steel solebar, round-section truss-rod, stepboards and dynamo. Horsted Keynes, 7th April, 1991. *Author*

1949. From mid-1956 green became the standard Southern Region livery. No. 400 was so repainted at Lancing in August 1959.

In 1955, Nos. 937, 943, 952, 956 and 979 were roofboarded 'Newspaper Traffic' for Waterloo–West of England services. Nos. 961, 966 and 972 were added by 1956. Workings shown for September 1960 indicate that only two of these vans were in traffic while the remainder stood spare. Except on Monday mornings, one van ran from Waterloo to Salisbury in the 1.15 am newspaper train, then in the 3.17 am Salisbury to Weymouth and 11.30 am Weymouth to Waterloo. Each van worked on alternate days, but, by 1964, 4-wheel vans were no longer used for newspaper traffic.

Workings of BY Stove vans Nos. 400/1 in September 1960 were as shown:

	1 van
2.6 am	Freight Exeter Central to Tavistock North
10.55 pm	Empty stock Tavistock North to Plymouth (SX)
6.48 pm	Passenger Tavistock North to Plymouth (SO)
	1 van
12.55 am	Freight Plymouth to Yeoford
3.20 am	Vans Yeoford to Exeter Ctl (MX), Exmouth Junction (MO)
4.04 am	Freight Exmouth Junction to Axminster, Mondays only
1.55 pm	Passenger Axminster to Exeter Central. Mondays only

Nos. 402–8, the only other stove-fitted BY allocated to the South Western Division, were spare. Nos. 409–19 were allocated to the Central Division. In 1966 Nos. 420–30 were also fitted with stoves and the allocation was now: 400–6/20–30 South Western Division and 407–19 Central Division. Of these, 16 were in traffic on the SWD, 11 on the CD and four spare for maintenance.

On the Central Division, several van trains included a stove-fitted guard's van in their formation. In 1954 a stove BY was formed in the 3.25 am paper train from London Bridge to Brighton, continuing to Eastbourne at 5.00 am. It returned from Eastbourne to Brighton at 10.05 am and to London Bridge in the 11.18 pm parcels train. From November 1959 there was a separate London Bridge to Eastbourne newspaper train leaving at 3.27 am and this included a BY. The van returned to London Bridge on the 6.00 pm East-bourne to Tunbridge Wells West, 7.47 pm thence to East Croydon, which it left on the 9.45 pm parcels train to London Bridge. A year later there was a Stove BY on the 5.20 am Victoria to Eastbourne service; it was detached at Eridge and forwarded to Brighton. Another worked in the 7.31 am East-bourne to Tunbridge Wells West, where it was attached to the 9.24 am service to Victoria. Two BY vans often worked up to Victoria in the 1.55 pm train from Brighton via Eridge.

In the 1967–8 timetable ten stove brakes were diagrammed to work on Central Division van trains and each van had a working number to indicate that the diagram was to be adhered to as far as possible. The diagrams shown below include the working numbers (Mondays to Fridays only).

	dep.		dep.	
800		**805**		
Brighton	4.55 am MX	Redhill	12.18 pm MO	
Worthing Central	6.15 am Ety	London Bridge	–	
Littlehampton	7.03 pm	London Bridge	4.00 am MX	Ety
Chichester	7.50 pm	New Cross Gate	–	
Victoria	–			
801		**808**		
Eastbourne	8.18 pm	New Cross Gate	11.35 am Ety	
Brighton	11.18 pm	London Bridge	1.02 pm	
East Croydon	–	Brighton	11.18 pm	
		London Bridge	–	
802		**809**		
London Bridge	4.00 am Ety	East Croydon	⎰12.58 am MO	
New Cross Gate	7.20 pm Ety		⎱ 1.30 am MX	
London Bridge	10.40 pm	Victoria	6.00 am Ety	
Brighton	–	New Cross Gate	7.40 pm Ety	
		Victoria	9.32 pm	
		Haywards Heath	1.00 am	
		Eastbourne	–	
803		**818**		
Victoria	3.20 am	Three Bridges	12.45 am	
Brighton	5.47 pm	Chichester	11.35 am	
Victoria	–	London Bridge	4.15 pm Ety	
		New Cross Gate	–	
804		**820**		
Victoria	3.27 am	London Bridge	4.00 am TO Ety	
Eastbourne	8.18 pm	New Cross Gate	7.20 pm Ety	
Brighton	11.18 pm	London Bridge	10.40 pm	
London Bridge	–	Three Bridges	–	

MO: Mondays only
MX: Mondays excepted
TO: Tuesdays only

Brake vans without stoves also worked on the Central Division parcels trains: Working Nos. 806, 807, 810–7, 819 and 821–5.

On the South Eastern Division in 1966 there was no allocation of BY stove brakes, but there were 11 non-stove brakes in traffic plus two spare at Bricklayers Arms. One van worked in the 3.40 am Victoria to Dover Marine, returning empty to Bricklayers Arms next day; another worked in the 3.00 am Victoria to Ramsgate as far as Sittingbourne, thence Sheerness, returning empty to Bricklayers Arms the same day. The 3.00 am van was loaded with newspapers for Sittingbourne, Queenborough and Sheerness as well as parcels for Sheerness. The 3.40 am van conveyed parcels for Dover and foreign post. The 4.50 am London Bridge to Tonbridge included a BY for Dover which was loaded with fish for Ashford and for Dover.

DIAGRAM No. 3092

PASSENGER BRAKE VAN 'C'

NOS. 400-49, 651-800, 931-80.

TARE 16 TONS
LOAD 10 TONS

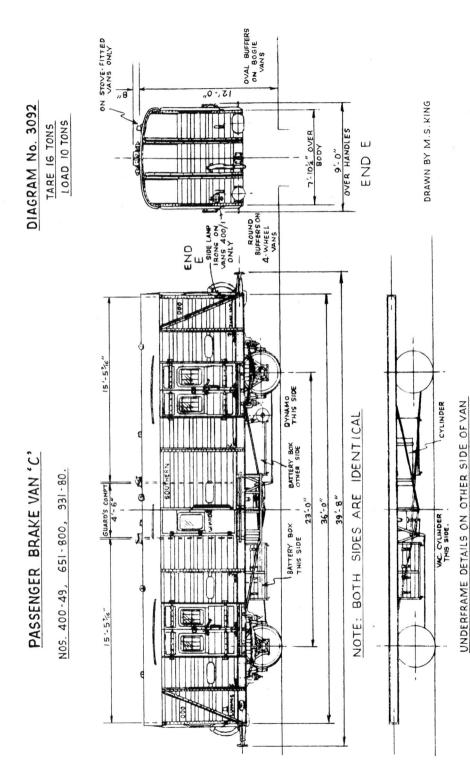

ON STOVE-FITTED VANS ONLY

OVAL BUFFERS ON BOGIE VANS

8"

12'-0"

7'-10¼" OVER BODY

9'-0" OVER HANDLES

END E

SIDE LAMP IRONS ON VANS 400/1 ONLY

ROUND BUFFERS ON 4-WHEEL VANS

END E

15'-5⅞6"

GUARD'S COMPT

4'-6"

15'-5⅞6"

BATTERY BOX THIS SIDE

DYNAMO THIS SIDE

BATTERY BOX OTHER SIDE

23'-0"

36'-0"

39'-8"

SOUTHERN

NOTE: BOTH SIDES ARE IDENTICAL

VAC. CYLINDER THIS SIDE.

CYLINDER

UNDERFRAME DETAILS ON OTHER SIDE OF VAN

DRAWN BY M. S. KING

Another use for BY vans, though rare, was as temporary substitute for a brake coach when it was necessary to withdraw such a vehicle from a set train for repairs. During May 1961 4-coach set No. 183 was running with three coaches and a 4-wheel brake van.

All the vans in the 400–30 series had their stoves removed in 1969.

From 1967 vans began to be repainted in BR's new livery of matt blue (which was applied to the ends as well as the sides) with all lettering in white. However, their days were numbered as brake vans, for in 1969 they had their lighting removed and were shown in lists as 'former brake vans'. They were now regarded as parcels vans and, as such, often worked off the Southern Region. Cambridge alone saw visits by No. 416 on 17th May, 1969; No. 699 on 24th July, 1969 and No. 959 on 6th August, 1969.

Apart from one van, No. 777, which had suffered accident damage at Witham, Eastern Region, on 7th March, 1950 and was cut up on the spot, withdrawals began with No. 797 in May 1966 and continued steadily throughout the late 1960s and early 1970s until by 1976 very few were left. The very last SR BY to be withdrawn was No. 713, in August 1978.

These vans have not found much favour for conversion into departmental service vehicles, only 14 having been so used, plus a few 'Internal User' examples. Several have been preserved by private railways, however.

404 To SE Steam Centre, Ashford c. 1972; Bluebell Rly 5.1978
407 To Conwy Valley Railway Museum, Bettws-y-coed, c. 1973
440 To Kent & East Sussex Railway, 7.1977
442 To Bluebell Railway, 7.1970. Has seen use on passenger trains
653 To Bluebell Railway, 11.1973
765 To Mid-Hants Railway, 10.1976
798 To Yorkshire Dales Railway, 1978
931 To Llangollen Railway, 1978

Safe-fitted guard's van No. 12, built by Lancing (*underframe*) and Eastleigh (*body*) in April 1941. The safe may be seen just to the right of the guard's door. Numbers painted in large white figures on a red panel. Exeter Central, 23rd August, 1964.

P.H. Swift

4-WHEELED BRAKE VANS
Summary of Building and Withdrawal Dates

Built		Withdrawn	Built		Withdrawn
10	4.41	11.76	436	7.37 To DB975140,	–
11	4.41 Eastleigh	12.77		1971	
12	4.41 Cardiff	7.78	7	6.37 Eastleigh	4.78
13	4.41 Bricklayers Arms	4.78	8	7.37	9.72
14	4.41	9.69	9	7.37	1.73
400	7.37	6.69	440	7.37 Eastleigh	4.77
1	7.37	9.72	1	6.37	7.77
2	6.37	2.72	2	6.37	6.69
3	6.37	6.69	3	6.37	76
4	6.37	6.71	4	7.37 Parkeston Quay	5.78
5	6.37 To DB975143,	–	5	7.37	7.69
	1971		6	7.37	1.68
6	6.37	5.69	7	7.37	10.71
7	6.37	1.73	8	7.37	3.72
8	6.37 To DB975141,	–	9	7.37	4.72
	1971		651	9.38	9.68
9	6.37	2.69	2	9.38 Peterborough	7.78
410	6.37 Worcester	7.78	3	9.38	6.72
1	6.37	9.68	4	8.38	1.67
2	6.37 To 083356,	c.89	5	8.38	c.11.77
	11.78		6	9.38	9.73
3	6.37 Bricklayers Arms	4.78	7	8.38	9.71
4	6.37	8.72	8	9.38	3.69
5	7.37	11.68	9	9.38 Bricklayers Arms	6.78
6	7.37	11.71	660	8.38	76
7	6.37 Basingstoke	7.78	1	9.38	8.69
8	7.37	6.69	2	8.38 Clapham Jn	7.78
9	7.37 To ADB975548,	–	3	8.38 Clapham Jn	3.78
	1976		4	8.38	9.72
420	6.37 Clapham Jn	6.78	5	8.38 Bradford	4.78
1	6.37	76	6	9.38	4.69
2	6.37	9.72	7	8.38 Willesden	6.78
3	6.37 To DB975311,	–	8	8.38	3.69
	1973		9	8.38	2.72
4	6.37	5.69	670	8.38	11.71
5	6.37	1.73	1	4.38	11.68
6	6.37	c.9.77	2	3.38 Manchester Red Bk	6.78
7	6.37	by 8.78	3	3.38 Cardiff Canton	7.78
8	7.37	78	4	3.38	12.68
9	7.37	c.9.77	5	3.38 Ipswich	5.78
430	7.37	3.69	6	3.38	2.69
1	7.37 Accident damage,	1.73	7	3.38	by 8.78
	Woking		8	3.38	by 8.78
2	7.37 Old Oak Common	7.78	9	3.38 Eastleigh	4.77
3	6.37	3.69	680	3.38	1.69
4	6.37 To DB975282,	–	1	3.38	3.69
	1973		2	3.38 Ports & Southsea	7.78
5	6.37 To ADB975672,	–	3	3.38 To DB975807,	–
	1978			1978	

Built		Withdrawn	Built		Withdrawn
684	3.38	6.69	728	5.38	5.69
5	3.38	1.69	9	5.38	11.76
6	3.38	5.69	730	5.38 Clapham Jn	6.78
7	3.38 To DB975160, then	c.80	1	6.38	76
	DS70323, 1971		2	4.38 To 083330,	c.89
8	3.38 Parkeston Quay	5.78		4.78	
9	3.38	7.69	3	4.38	78
690	3.38	1.77	4	4.38	5.69
1	3.38 Acton	7.78	5	6.38	11.76
2	4.38	1.67	6	6.38	5.69
3	4.38	by 8.78	7	6.38 Bricklayers Arms	4.78
4	4.38	11.76	8	6.38	11.71
5	4.38	7.72	9	6.38	7.77
6	4.38	76	740	6.38 Newcastle	8.78
7	4.38 Clapham Jn	7.78	1	6.38	12.68
8	6.38 Eastleigh	7.78	2	6.38	5.69
9	6.38 To 083355,	c.89	3	6.38	4.78
	11.78		4	4.38	11.71
700	6.38 To DB975283,	–	5	4.38	9.71
	1973		6	4.38 To ADB975671,	c.82
1	3.38 Cardiff Canton	7.78		1978	
2	3.38	5.69	7	4.38	3.72
3	4.38	1.69	8	6.38	10.68
4	4.38	76	9	6.38	6.69
5	4.38	76	750	6.38	9.71
6	3.38	12.72	1	6.39	c.77
7	3.38 Llanelli	7.78	2	7.39	11.68
8	3.38 Wolverton	6.78	3	7.39	77
9	3.38	3.69	4	3.39	76
710	4.38	11.76	5	3.39	9.66
1	6.38 Peterborough	5.78	6	3.39	11.71
2	6.38 To DB975142,	–	7	3.39	3.69
	1971		8	6.39	7.69
3	5.38	8.78	9	7.39 Birmingham Crzn St	6.78
4	4.38 Clapham Jn	3.78	760	7.39	1.69
5	3.38 Bricklayers Arms	6.78	1	7.39	7.69
6	7.38	by 8.78	2	7.39 Basingstoke	7.78
7	4.38	7.77	3	10.39	5.69
8	4.38	77	4	10.39 To DB975284,	–
9	5.38	9.72		1973	
720	5.38 Hitchin	6.78	5	7.39	76
1	6.38	by 8.78	6	7.39	10.71
2	6.38 Clapham Jn	5.78	7	7.39	76
3	8.38 Southampton Dks	6.78	8	7.39	3.66
4	6.38	12.68	9	6.39	78
5	7.38	10.68	770	10.39 Eastleigh	2.78
6	5.38	11.76	1	8.39	5.69
7	3.38	c.76	2	4.39	3.69

Built	Withdrawn	Built	Withdrawn
773 4.39	4.66	941 11.40	76
4 3.39 Poole	4.78	2 1.41	11.68
5 4.39	7.77	3 12.40	5.69
6 7.39	76	4 10.40 Eastleigh	6.78
7 8.39 Accident damage Witham, 7.3.50. Broken up on site	3.50	5 11.40 Eastleigh	6.78
		6 12.40 Bricklayers Arms	6.78
		7 11.40 Ferme Park	7.78
8 8.39 Parkeston Quay	5.78	8 11.40	76
9 8.39	9.68	9 12.40	4.69
780 7.39	1.69	950 1.41 Manchester Red Bk	7.78
1 10.39	1.69	1 12.40	c.77
2 10.39	7.69	2 1.41	5.69
3 10.39	7.77	3 11.40	6.69
4 6.39	11.76	4 12.40	10.68
5 7.39	8.69	5 11.40	9.69
6 8.39	7.69	6 12.40	5.69
7 3.39 Clapham Jn	7.78	7 12.40 Haverfordwest	7.78
8 3.39	10.68	8 10.40 Bristol	4.78
9 3.39 Norwood Jn	5.78	9 12.40 Bricklayers Arms	7.78
790 7.39	1.78	960 1.41	11.76
1 7.39	77	1 12.40	11.69
2 7.39	5.72	2 12.40	1.69
3 4.39	4.69	3 12.40	77
4 5.39	11.71	4 11.40 To DB975144, 1971	–
5 6.39	1.77		
6 5.39	9.68	5 12.40	11.76
7 5.39	5.66	6 12.40 Cardiff Canton	7.78
8 5.39 Bradford Exch.	3.78	7 12.40	2.69
9 5.39	2.69	8 12.40 Fratton	7.78
800 5.39	5.69	9 11.40 York	6.78
931 11.40 Manchester Red Bk	2.78	970 12.40	2.69
2 10.40	5.69	1 1.41	5.69
3 12.40 Cardiff Canton	7.78	2 11.40 Cleethorpes	7.78
4 1.41	2.69	3 1.41	1.69
5 10.40	4.69	4 1.41	5.69
6 12.40	8.69	5 10.40 Andover	7.78
7 12.40	6.69	6 11.40	2.69
8 1.41	12.71	7 12.40 Preston	5.78
9 10.40	12.68	8 11.40 Eastleigh	2.78
940 10.40 Damaged Willesden 7.73	3.74	9 11.40	2.69
		980 11.40	11.68

Notes

DB975141: burnt out, 1989.
No. 938 dual heated and fitted with lavatory, 1967.

Chapter Three
Bogie Guard's Vans

The Southern bogie guard's van was perhaps the handsomest of the whole range of non-passenger-carrying vehicle designs, even though it was hardly likely to have been planned as anything other than functional. Effectively it was a 'stretched' version of the 1937-built 4-wheeled guard's van, with the same style of body planking and the same sets of double doors each fitted with a droplight.

Fifty vans were authorised in March 1936, originally intended to be bogie luggage vans but later revised to include a guard's compartment. Construction, to Order No. A927, was carried out at Eastleigh (bodies) and Ashford Works (underframes) and the vans (Diagram No. 3093) were sent into traffic between August and October 1938, coded as 'Van B'.

Each van was 50 ft over headstocks (53 ft 8½ in. over buffers), 12 ft high from rail to roof (12 ft 8 in. over guard's periscope) and 8 ft 9 in. wide. A centrally-placed guard's compartment 4 ft 6 in. wide – exactly the same as on the 4-wheeled vans – was flanked by two large luggage compartments each 22 ft 5⁷⁄₁₆ in. long. There were four sets of double doors on each bodyside but no fixed windows in the body, nor were there end gangways. Body planking was arranged in alternate pairs of wide and narrow horizontal boards. Vehicle numbers were 350–99, and each van weighed 28 tons.

Another batch of 50 vans, to Order No. L1029, was built at Eastleigh on Lancing underframes in November and December 1939, these being numbered 201–50. Livery was green bodyside, with black ends, underframe and bogies, and grey roof.

These vans soon put in an appearance on the London West carriage working notice, which showed several formed in newspaper trains – with which they were to be associated for very many years. From September 1938 the 1.30 am Waterloo–West of England service included a Van B for Padstow, one for Exeter and one for Torrington, in replacement of ex-London & South Western bogie vans. A van worked through in the 3.20 am Waterloo to Portsmouth Harbour, and the 5.40 am Waterloo to Weymouth had one that worked as far as Southampton Central. Another was formed in the 10.30 pm Waterloo to Dorchester train, detached at Eastleigh for Portsmouth & Southsea.

By March 1941, when several night trains had been arranged to start their westward journeys from stations short of London, the 1.40 am Wimbledon to Plymouth etc. had one Van B for Padstow, one for Torrington and one for Salisbury which then worked to Weymouth at 3.52 am. The 3.15 am from Surbiton had a van for Portsmouth Harbour, one for Portsmouth & Southsea and one for Bournemouth West. The 10.45 pm from Surbiton to Dorchester included a Van B for Portsmouth & Southsea via Eastleigh.

No Van B appears to have been allocated to the Eastern Section until about 1946, and normally the vans did not work off the Western Section of the Southern Railway. However, No. 360 somehow found its way to Swansea in September 1940 and there its roof planking was damaged; later it was sent to Eastleigh for repairs. Other vans damaged in wartime were Nos. 216 and 365 on 8th September, 1940, when a high-explosive bomb fell on Clapham

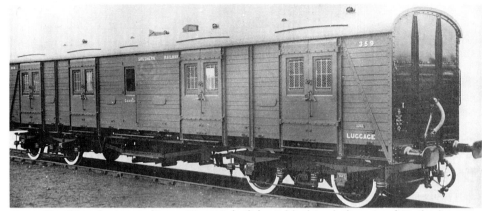

Van 'B', or bogie guard's van, No. 359, built by Ashford (*underframe*) and Eastleigh (*body*) in September 1938. The doors and the body planking are the same as those on the 4-wheeled vans.   *Author's Collection*

Stove-fitted Van 'B', as indicated by the orange panels in the top corners and on the guard's door. No. 381, built Ashford/Estleigh in August 1938, received a stove in about 1946. Eastleigh, 29th October, 1949.   *A.E. West*

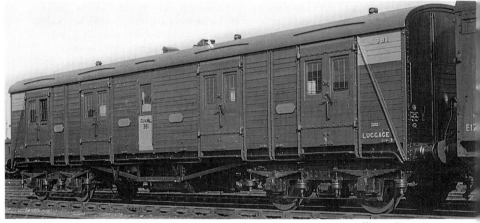

Van 'B' in the number series 265–280 allocated to newspaper traffic and carrying roofboards lettered 'Newspaper Traffic – Waterloo Padstow'. This van was one of the batch built at Lancing in 1952.   *M.S. King*

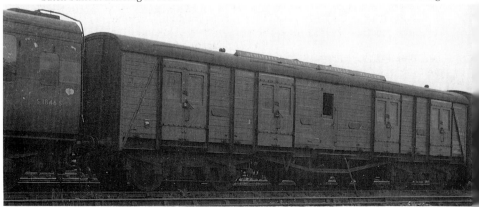

Junction carriage shed; and No. 242 on 12th January, 1941, when a fire caused by incendiaries at Rotherhithe Road carriage depot severely scorched this van. All were returned into traffic after repairs.

By 1944 Nos. 395–9 had been fitted with stoves (in addition to steam heaters, with which all the vans were originally equipped) and two years later Nos. 380–94 had also been so-fitted. Like the stove-fitted 4-wheeled vans, the bogie vans were distinguished by orange panels painted on the top left and top right bodysides and a similar panel on the guard's door. Special workings were published for stove-fitted vans, which were not to work off the Southern Railway. Ten more had received stoves by 1950, these being Nos. 370–79; two more, Nos. 368/9, were equipped in 1962.

In the workings shown for October 1946 the 1.25 am from Waterloo had a Van B for Padstow, one for Yeovil and one for Weymouth via Salisbury. The 2.40 am from Waterloo had two vans for Portsmouth Harbour and the 3.45 am Portsmouth train had one detached at Petersfield. That town was also the destination of a van formed in the 7.00 pm from Waterloo, detached at Woking and forwarded at 4.35 am next morning.

A final batch of 30 vans was built at Lancing during 1952/3, identical to the pre-War batches – although slight variations in body planking might have been detected by the keen-eyed. Vehicle numbers were S 251 S to S 280 S (Order No. 3227) and the vans emerged in BR crimson livery.

Between 1949 and 1955 a bogie stove brake was booked to run in each of the following Eastern Section train services: 3.00 am Holborn Viaduct to Ramsgate vans, 11.00 am Holborn Viaduct to Ramsgate vans, 3.40 am London Bridge to Hastings, plus one for Dover (later Sandwich) detached at Tonbridge; 11.50 pm London Bridge to Deal; and the 3.30 am Victoria to Ramsgate vans. There were still no bogie brake vans allocated to Central Section workings.

Examples of workings of stove-fitted bogie brake vans on the Western Section in 1960/1 (one per train) are quoted below. The allocation was Nos. 380–99, with 18 in traffic and two spare.

Wkg 92		3.54 pm Clapham Junction to Exeter Central milk empties
Wkg 93		2.06 am Exeter Ctl – Torrington freight; 2.47 pm Torrington to Crediton; 5.35 pm to Exeter Central vans and milk tanks; thence to Clapham Junction at 6.48 pm. Workings 92 and 93 were on alternate days.
Wkg 102/104	(alternate days)	2.15 am Eastleigh to Weymouth vans and 7.54 pm return.
Wkg 103		1.50 am (Mondays excepted) Basingstoke to Yeovil Town vans and 5.35 pm (Saturdays excepted) Yeovil Town to Clapham Junction vans.

Other bogie vans with special workings were those allocated exclusively to newspaper traffic and were so-distinguished by roofboards which read: 'Newspaper Traffic' (first board) 'Waterloo Padstow', or whichever destination was appropriate (second board). Nos. 265–80, so-fitted in 1953/4, were the actual vehicles and of these 14 were in traffic, each on a 2-day diagram, and two stood spare. These were the 1960/1 workings:

Wkg 69, 70 alt.

	dep.
Waterloo	1.15 am
Padstow	3.13 pm
Waterloo	

Wkg 71, 72 alt.

Waterloo	1.15 am
Torrington	8.53 am
Exeter Ctl	11.45 am
Exmouth	4.00 pm
Sidmouth Jn	5.18 pm Freight
Waterloo	–

Wkg 73, 74 alt.

Waterloo	1.15 am
Torrington	8.53 am
Exeter Ctl	11.47 am
Bude	3.17 pm
Waterloo	–

Wkg 75, 76 alt.

	dep.
Waterloo	1.15 am
Salisbury	3.20 am
Yeovil Town	4.06 pm
Waterloo	–

Wkg 77, 78 alt.

Waterloo	1.15 am
Ilfracombe	3.00 pm
Waterloo	–

Wkg 68, 79 alt.

Waterloo	1.15 am
Salisbury	3.17 am
Weymouth	8.25 am
Bournemouth Ctl	Ety
Bournemouth W.	4.55 pm
Waterloo	–

Wkg 80, 81 alt.

Waterloo	1.15 am
Yeovil Town	3.00 pm
Waterloo	–

By 1964 the vans were no longer roofboarded, merely stencilled 'Newspaper Traffic', and only Nos. 272–80 were so marked. These remained in use until May 1975, when only Nos. 272–7 were allocated; and two years later only Nos. 276/7 were still stencilled 'Newspaper Traffic', one or the other working in the 3.35 am Victoria to Hastings via Tonbridge van train.

The stove-fitted brakes, Nos. 368–99, were in 1961 divided between the South Eastern Division (368–83) and the South Western Division (384–99). Not until 1966 did the Central Division receive any. In order for this to happen, further vehicles needed to be stove-fitted, and in 1966/7 Nos. 201–3/5–30 were converted. The allocation was now: Central Division 222–30; South Eastern Division 210–21; 368–83; and South Western Division 201–3/5–9, 384–92/4–9. No. 393 had been withdrawn in March 1966. On the CD there were seven diagrammed, on the SED 24, and on the SWD 19, leaving ten for maintenance spares. In addition, No. 231 was stove-fitted in 1968 and allocated to the Central Division.

A South Eastern Division working book dated 6th June, 1966 shows not only van workings but also with what the vans themselves were to be loaded. The Stove B formed in the 4.50 am London Bridge to Margate conveyed parcels and parcel post for Ramsgate and Margate and letter mail for intermediate stations. Another Stove Van B in the same train, detached at Dover Priory, carried letters for Dover and parcels for intermediate stations.

Lancing-built Van 'B' No. 278 seen at Reading on 20th June, 1971. The planking on the doors differs from that found on the vans built in 1938/9, and the 'V'-hanger is at the right-hand instead of the left-hand end of the truss-rod. *Author*

Van 'B' No. 358 (Ashford/Eastleigh, September 1938) at Clapham Junction on 3rd March, 1978, by which time the guard's compartment was no longer in use and the van was running as an ordinary luggage van. *Author*

PASSENGER BRAKE VAN 'B'

NOS. 201-80, 350-99.

DIAGRAM No. 3093

TARE 28 TONS

DRAWN BY M. S. KING

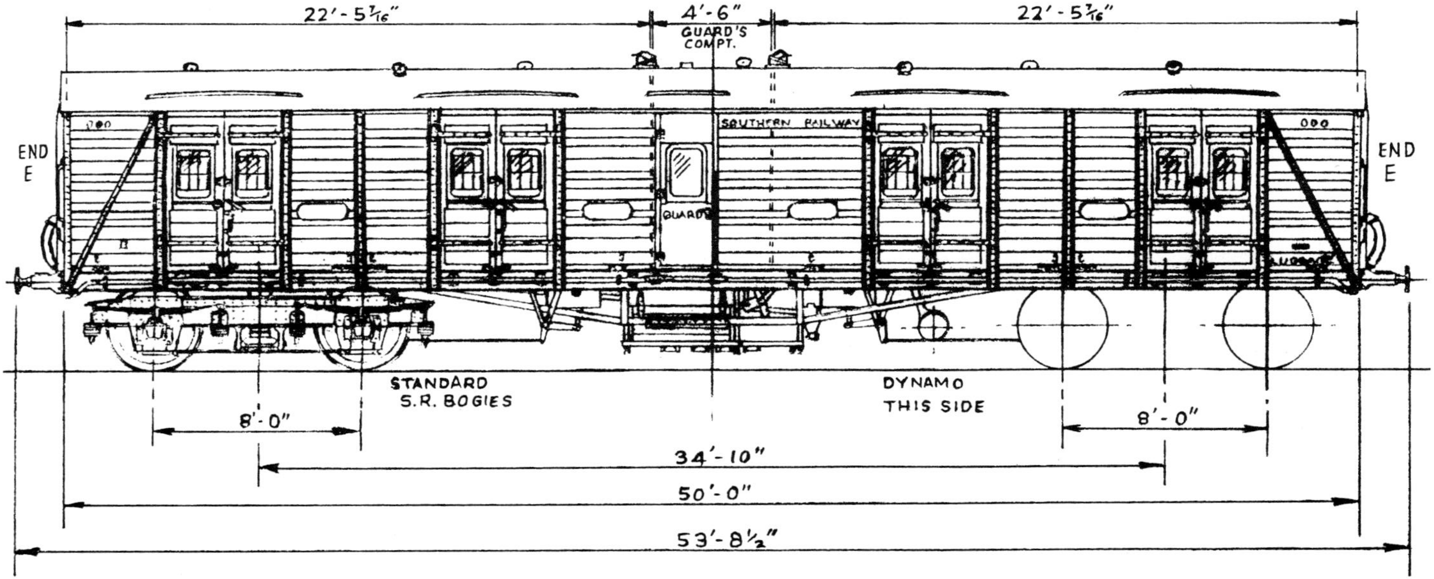

NOTE : BOTH SIDES ARE IDENTICAL

END E

END E

GUARD'S COMPT.

GUARD

SOUTHERN RAILWAY

DYNAMO THIS SIDE

STANDARD S.R. BOGIES

22'-5 7/16"

4'-6"

22'-5 7/16"

8'-0"

8'-0"

34'-10"

50'-0"

53'-8 1/2"

The 3.00 am Victoria to Ramsgate passenger and paper train included a B Stove for Gillingham, carrying the Dartford, Gillingham and Rainham news. The 3.40 am Victoria to Dover had a B Stove for Hastings detached at Tonbridge; it conveyed letter mail, news and parcel post for Hastings and newspapers for St Leonards and Rye. It was a marvel of organisation to see that the right vans were loaded with the correct items and unloaded at the proper stations.

From July 1967, these were the workings of bogie stove brakes in van trains on the Central Division, Mondays to Fridays.

203	dep.		**214**	dep.	
Three Bridges	12.45 am	MX	London Bridge	5.30 am	MX
Chichester	7.50 pm		Brighton	11.18 pm	
Victoria	–		London Bridge	–	

207			**227**		
Victoria	3.40 am	Ety	East Croydon	⌠12.58 am	MO
New Cross Gate	11.35 am	Ety		⌡ 1.30 am	MX
London Bridge	1.02 pm		Victoria	6.00 am	Ety
Brighton	11.18 pm		New Cross Gate	7.40 pm	Ety
East Croydon	–		Victoria	9.32 pm	
			Three Bridges	–	

There were also 24 non-stove vans diagrammed on Central Division parcels trains, Mondays to Fridays.

After the red livery that BR introduced in 1949 came the restoration of green in all repaints from mid-1956; then in 1967 vans began to be sprayed with matt blue, ends and all, and given tiny white lettering. However, whatever the colour, the vans looked just the same as they had always done because of the liberal coating of grime that covered them after some months in traffic. They were seldom cleaned. No. S 270 S had received its blue livery when it turned up at Cambridge on 16th May, 1969.

From 1969 the guard's compartments were disused and the lighting was stripped. The accommodation standards had fallen below what guards were accustomed to, and the men had been refusing to ride in the vans, which were now shown in lists as 'former brake vans'. Only No. 204 remained a brake van, but this was on loan to the Scottish Region in 1969. That year was also when all but six of the stove brakes lost that designation, only Nos. 225–30 remaining stove-fitted for use on the South Eastern Division until 1974. Few vans had been scrapped, even by 1976, as they were still useful purely as parcels and news vans. On 2nd June, 1976 No. 363 was noted in the 1.40 am Waterloo to Yeovil train, conveying the Salisbury news and parcels.

Bogie vans could also be seen off the Southern Region: on 6th July, 1978, No. S 353 was noted in the 5.14 am Bristol to Weymouth passenger train, returning at 9.15 am. But this was nothing compared with their ranging far and wide in Scotland: on 6th June, 1978, a Van B was on the rear of the 8.00 pm King's Cross to Aberdeen (believed detached at Edinburgh) and on the previous day one was seen formed in the 9.40 pm Edinburgh to Carstairs.

Serious inroads on the bogie vans began to be made in the early 1980s, and a small number were transferred to departmental use. With the decline in parcels traffic, they became, like so much else on BR, 'surplus to requirements' and the remainder were withdrawn in bulk in 1986, the last examples being Nos. 252/65/76 in August 1986 and No. 254 in September following.

No. 201 was acquired by the North Downs Steam Railway, a small concern that by 1988 had built a short length of railway at the top of a hill at Stone Lodge, North Kent. No. 385 was purchased by the Swanage Railway and had arrived there by 1987.

BOGIE GUARD'S VANS
Summary of Building and Withdrawal Dates

Built			Withdrawn	Built			Withdrawn
201	12.39	Clapham Jn	5.81	230	12.39		81
2	11.39		c.3.81	1	12.39		9.72
3	11.39	To 041508, 8.80	–	2	12.39	To ADB977065, 82	c.89
4	11.39	Doncaster	9.80	3	11.39		c.3.81
5	11.39	To 083571, 7.84	c.89	4	11.39	Clapham Jn	5.81
6	11.39		c.78	5	11.39		10.82
7	11.39		c.10.80	6	11.39		8.86
8	12.39	Clapham Jn	5.81	7	11.39	Upperby	6.81
9	12.39		c.10.80	8	11.39		c.7.79
210	12.39	To 083618, c.89	–	9	11.39		76
1	11.39		81	240	11.39	Clapham Jn	6.81
2	11.39	New Cross Gate	5.86	1	11.39		c.10.81
3	11.39	Clapham Jn	5.81				
4	11.39	Doncaster	9.78	242	11.39	To 083596, c.85	–
5	11.39	Clapham Jn	5.81	3	11.39		c.10.80
6	11.39		4.86	4	11.39	Doncaster	9.80
7	11.39	Bristol	1.81	5	11.39	New Cross Gate	5.86
8	11.39		c.3.81	6	11.39	Clapham Jn	9.81
9	11.39	To 083572, 7.84	c.89	7	11.39		c.5.81
220	11.39	To 024450, 8.82	–	8	11.39	To ADB977112, 82	–
1	11.39	Bricklayers Arms	5.81	9	11.39	To ADB977066, 82	84
2	11.39	To ADB977111, 82	–	250	12.39		11.76
3	11.39		c.4.81	1	1952	New Cross Gate	5.86
4	11.39		c.10.80	2	,,		8.86
5	11.39	Bricklayers Arms	5.81	3	,,		8.81
6	11.39	Doncaster	10.78	4	,,		9.86
7	12.39		81	5	,,	New Cross Gate	5.86
8	12.39		c.11.81	6	,,	New Cross Gate	5.86
9	11.39		76	7	,,	Clapham Jn	5.81
				8	,,		1.83
				9	,,	Clapham Jn	5.81

Built	Withdrawn	Built	Withdrawn
260 1952 New Cross Gate	5.86	370 10.38	10.84
1 ,, New Cross Gate	5.86	1 9.38	c.10.80
2 ,,	c.85	2 10.38 Basingstoke	84
3 ,, Clapham Jn	5.81	3 10.38	10.85
4 ,, New Cross Gate	6.86	4 9.38	2.67
5 ,,	8.86	5 10.38	81
6 ,, Doncaster	9.78	6 9.38	c.10.80
7 ,, Clapham Jn	6.81	7 9.38 Bricklayers Arms	5.81
8 ,, Clapham Jn	5.81	8 9.38 Bricklayers Arms	5.81
9 ,, Clapham Jn	5.81	9 8.38 To 083336,	c.89
270 ,, New Cross Gate	5.86	10.80	
1 ,, Clapham Jn	5.81	380 8.38 Whittlesea	3.81
2 ,, New Cross Gate	5.86	1 8.38 Doncaster	3.81
3 ,, New Cross Gate	5.86	2 8.38 To ADB977067,	c.89
4 ,, New Cross Gate	6.86	82	
5 ,, Clapham Jn	5.81	3 8.38	c.4.81
6 ,,	8.86	4 8.38	12.67
7 ,,	c.2.81	5 8.38	c.11.81
8 ,,	2.82	6 9.38	c.7.81
9 ,,	c.3.81	7 8.38	by 4.76
280 ,,	5.81	8 8.38	c.10.80
350 8.38	81	9 8.38	76
1 8.38	76	390 8.38	c.10.80
2 8.38 Clapham Jn	5.81	1 8.38	c.7.81
3 8.38 Doncaster	9.80	2 8.38 To 061054,	—
4 8.38	c.4.80	3.86	
5 8.38 Clapham Jn	5.81	3 9.38	3.66
356 8.38 Clapham Jn	6.81	4 9.38	81
7 9.38 Doncaster	9.80	5 8.38	by 5.75
8 9.38	c5.81	6 9.38 To ADB977011,	—
9 9.38 Doncaster	9.78	82	
360 8.38 To TDB975402,	—	7 8.38	c.3.79
8.74		8 9.38	c.3.79
1 9.38	11.76	9 9.38	8.86
2 10.38 Clapham Jn	6.81		
3 8.38 New Cross Gate	5.86		
4 8.38	c.80		
5 10.38 Clapham Jn	5.81		
6 10.38	76		
7 10.38	3.66		
8 10.38 Bricklayers Arms	5.81	*Notes*	
9 10.38	5.84	TDB975402 re-numbered 083235, 6.75.	

A detailed view of the vacuum-brake cylinder and 'V'-hanger on former SE&C luggage van No. 153, owned by the Bluebell Railway. Horsted Keynes, 7th April, 1991.
Author

Laminated springs, 'W' irons, SR axlebox cover plate, paint-date on solebar and part of handbrake lever on luggage van No. 153 at Horsted Keynes, 7th April, 1991.
Author

Chapter Four
4-wheeled Luggage Vans

Many hundreds of standard SR luggage vans were built over the years. As a design it was extremely long-lived, although individual vehicles seldom remained in traffic for longer than 30 years. As with Great Western locomotives, SR vans all looked alike to the casual observer, but there were detail differences. Similarly there was a tendency to replace worn-out vans by new ones of similar appearance, just as the GW did its locomotives.

The design of the SR passenger luggage vans can be traced back to a single vehicle built by the South Eastern & Chatham Railway in 1919, and the last vans to make their appearance were constructed by British Railways in 1951. So either the design was very advanced for its time or the Southern had an excessively conservative policy when it came to rolling stock.

Ashford Works constructed a prototype passenger luggage van, quite unlike other SEC vans in appearance, during 1919. It had a body length of 32 ft (35 ft 10 in. over buffers) and employed a construction of light steel framework planked internally with wooden boards. It owed more to the technique of goods van building than of passenger coach construction. Body width was 7 ft 10¼ in. (8 ft 4¼ in. over stanchions). The height from rail to top of the roof was 12 ft and the wheelbase was 21 ft. Tare weight was 12 tons.

There were two sets of double doors on each bodyside and four fixed windows, behind which were three horizontal bars to protect the glass from damage by piled-up luggage. A lozenge-shaped panel used for chalking destinations was located below the two outer-end windows but not the two centre windows. On the roof (which had an elliptical profile and was made of wooden boards covered with canvas) were four torpedo ventilators and there was an angled steel ventilator cover in each body-end, top centre. Internally there were two interconnected luggage compartments of slightly unequal length, one being 15 ft 10 in. and the other 15 ft 11 in., with a hinged shelf at each end. The van was numbered 132 in the SEC passenger van list. Unlike any other 4-wheeled van on the SEC, it was exempt from the rule that such vans must not be marshalled between bogie vehicles.

Clearly the new van was satisfactory, for 20 more were ordered, a contract being placed with the Bristol Carriage & Wagon Co. They were delivered in 1921 and received the numbers 121–5, 136–50. The only difference between them and the prototype seems to be that there was now a chalking panel beneath all four windows on each bodyside. Finally, a further 24 vans were built by Ashford in mid-1922; both these and the Bristol vans tared 13 tons each. Filling up numbers vacated by withdrawn vehicles, these were given Nos. 152–5/7/8/60–3/6–70/2–5/7/9–82.

All 45 luggage vans appeared in the SEC livery of dark umber brown with bold yellow lettering. On coming into Southern ownership they were given the diagram number 960. First to be repainted in the new livery of sage green, with chrome lettering shaded black to right and base, was No. 132, the prototype, renumbered 1972 at Ashford in November 1925. All the rest were renumbered in the same order as the SEC numbering, becoming Nos. 1973 to

2016. The Bristol vehicles were all done at Ashford in 1925/6, and the 1922-built vans mostly in 1928/9 at Ashford and Lancing. No. 180 became No. 2014 at Eastleigh in January 1930, and No. 153 (the last to retain SEC livery) became No. 1994 in August 1930 at Ashford.

Many of these vans were used in Continental boat trains, two almost invariably being formed at the London end of each train. Some even were given roof brackets to hold wooden destination boards. Nos. 1972–91 were those specially allocated during 1934/5: one was in the 9.00 am Victoria to Folkestone Harbour and 3.40 pm return, another in the 10.05 am Victoria to Newhaven Harbour and 4.45 pm return.

For its first few years the Southern concentrated on building vans closely based on the SEC type but equipped with end-loading doors. However, despite the success of this type (the general utility van) it was still felt desirable to have some more ordinary luggage vans, and the first 50 were authorised in April 1933, Ashford Works being given the task of building them. Numbered 2181–2230, to SR Diagram No. 3103, they emerged between October 1934 and March 1935. They were very close copies of the SEC vans, the main difference being that, unlike them, the SR version had four bodyside ventilators, each protected by an angled steel hood, below each of the four chalk panels – which in turn were immediately below each window. The vans measured 35 ft 8 in. over buffers (2 inches shorter than the SEC overall length) but other dimensions were identical. Internal arrangements differed in that there were no partitions; the SR van's interior was an empty shell, the floor being of Decolite construction (cement and wire mesh).

A further 97 passenger luggage vans (PLV), to Order No. A824, came out of Ashford between April and December 1935, these receiving the numbers 1154–1250. They had been authorised in March 1934, and 100 more were authorised in March 1935 (Order No. A855) for construction by Ashford; these were sent into traffic between March 1936 and April 1937: Nos. 1054–1153. Another batch of 50, to Order No. A973, was authorised in March 1937 and Ashford built them between October and December 1938 – Nos. 1921–70.

Ashford Works was also responsible for building the last batch before the outbreak of World War II, Nos. 1251–1398 being completed during 1939. Of these, Nos. 1359–98 were the first PLVs to have the 'alternate wide-and-narrow' planked pairs first seen on Eastleigh-built vans two years previously; it would seem that Ashford was using up its stocks of 6½ in.-wide planks before going over to the new standard planking (Order No. A1031).

During the first few years of the War, construction of PL vans continued but, as Ashford no longer had the capacity to build any (having been turned over to war work), Eastleigh and Lancing Works became responsible for building them. Both these Works were undertaking war work in addition.

One hundred vans were turned out between February and August 1940 with Eastleigh bodies on Lancing underframes to Order No. L1092. Nos. 1821–1920 were given standard bodies with the planking arranged 3½ in., 3½ in., 6½ in., 6½ in., etc.

SR parcels and miscellaneous van No. 1284, built at Ashford in May 1939 with equal-width planking. The van is shown in typically-scruffy condition, the bodyside and even the glazing being covered with chalked destinations. *M.S. King*

Cycle van No. 1282, converted in 1951 for conveying bicycles between London and the Channel ports. The van was built at Ashford in April 1939; the stencilled bicycle in the top right-hand corner is prominent. Photographed at Eardley on 12th September, 1956. *H.C. Casserley*

Ashford-built PMV No. 1307 at East Croydon post-office siding, 12th May, 1978. Both vans had arrived on the 4.55 am from Bricklayers Arms, and would leave at 10.40 pm for Redhill. *Author*

The next batch, 120 vehicles numbered 1781–1820 and 2091–2170, was built wholly by Lancing and displayed a body style not used before or since. All the horizontal planking was 6½ in. wide with the exception of one narrow plank along the centre line of the vehicle. The strapping was most odd, comprising 'U'–section steel plates with a length of timber bolted to one angle of the 'U' and to the body planking. It was as if the 'U'-section on its own was not thought strong enough and the timber was added to strengthen the assembly. These vehicles, to Order No. L1191, were constructed during 1942.

When Lancing received an order for 48 more vans (L1659) it built them in the normal style with alternate pairs of wide and narrow planking and they were completed in 1943. The floors were wooden planked instead of being of Decolite construction. Nos. 1053, 1692–1730 and 2083–90 were the last vans (except for 10 experimental plastic-bodied ones) to be built until after the War, when production was restarted.

To give the workings of PL vans at this stage is not possible as, unlike coaches, vans did not usually work to precise diagrams. The safest thing to say is that the vans ran almost anywhere and on almost any sort of train: passenger, parcels or goods. They also worked off the Southern Railway on to 'foreign' lines, and this happened to an even greater extent after nationalisation.

Some vans were converted to work with push-and-pull trains, needing the fitting of additional hoses and piping for the air-control gear on locomotives and driving trailer coaches. The vans concerned were Nos. 1996, 2001, 2002, 2004 and 2005 – ex-SEC PLVs – and were converted about 1941. A non-fitted van could work with a push-and-pull train so long as it was the tail-load, whether the locomotive was pulling or pushing its 2-coach set, but only a fitted van could work *between* the locomotive and the trailer coaches.

PL van No. 1915, new in August 1940, was immediately appropriated for use as a stores van for the chief mechanical engineer's drawing office and numbered 1572S in the service vehicles list. It was returned to stock as No. 1915 in August 1945.

A few vans were damaged during the War. On 7th November, 1940 No. 1389 received some damage by enemy action at Bricklayers Arms; on 4th May, 1941, when Portsmouth was under attack from incendiaries, one of these caused heavy damage to No. 1823 and lesser damage to No. 1122; No. 1191 had its body wrecked at Cannon Street on 28th May, 1941; and No. 1315 was damaged on 19th February, 1944 near Merton Abbey when bombs fell on Messrs Lines' factory and sidings. All were later repaired or, in the case of the Cannon Street victim, given a new body. Nos. 1200, 1201, 1312, 1337 and 1915 had been withdrawn from stock by May 1941; No. 1201 had been transferred in June 1939 to the service vehicles list as 281S (a rail cleaning van marked 'Chief Electrical Engineer's Department Brighton') and No. 1915 was temporarily 1572S. Twenty-three passenger luggage vans were converted to mobile workshops during the War, and were never returned to stock.

It was in 1947 that Ashford Works resumed construction of PL vans, after receiving an order (No. A3229) to build 60. Numbered 1501–60, they

Passenger luggage van No. 1840 in the final SR livery style, lettered 'Southern'. The van, which was built at Lancing (*underframe*) and Eastleigh (*body*) in March 1940, displays the later style of body planking. Exeter Central, 22nd July, 1948.   *A.E. West*

One of the seven PLVs sent to the Isle of Wight, given Westinghouse air brakes and side lamp irons: No. 1048 (formerly 1720), which was built at Lancing in June 1943. Newport (IOW), 21st May, 1957.   *H.C. Casserley*

maintained the standard style of body planking (3½ in., 3½ in., 6½ in., 6½ in., etc.). They were the last vans to be turned out in Southern livery – which as this stage was malachite green with the word 'Southern' on the bodyside. By the time the next batch of vans emerged in 1950, British Railways red was the order of the day. Order No. A3590 was for 111 vans, and construction was divided between Ashford, Lancing and Eastleigh, presumably as a means of getting the vehicles into traffic˙quickly. Nos. 1561–1671 all had plywood bodies, giving them a cheap-and-nasty appearance, although the doors had normal planking for strength. BR code was PMV-parcels and miscellaneous vans. Ashford built all the underframes and in addition the bodies of Nos. 1561–9/72/4–80/4–7/9/91/2/4–1608/ 12–19/23/29–32/46/7/59.

Eastleigh built the bodies of Nos. 1570/1/3/81–3, 1609–11/20–2/4/5/53.

Lancing built the bodies of Nos. 1588/90/3, 1626–8/33–45/8–52/4–8/ 60–71.

The final series of SR-style passenger luggage vans was built at Wolverton, the old London & North Western carriage works. At this date it was most unusual for one of the railway Regions to build vehicles for another Region. It is even possible that the wrong sets of drawings were sent to Wolverton, for instead of the current style of plywood vans those that emerged in 1951 had the older 6½ in./3½ in. alternate pairs of planks style. The fifty vans were numbered 1451–1500, the numbers having an S prefix and suffix and the livery being red.

In October 1950 seven PL vans were shipped across to the Isle of Wight, where they became renowned as the most modern stock on the Island. Did a parcel travel in greater comfort than a passenger on the Isle of Wight? Perhaps not. For use with the Island's trains the brakes on the vans had to be converted from vacuum to Westinghouse air, and side lamp irons were fitted to allow the vans to work in goods trains. In addition the vans were re-numbered in the Isle of Wight number series.

New No.	Old No.	Built	New No.	Old No.	Built
1046	1134	1937	1050	1321	1939
1047	1283	1939	1051	1384	1939
1048	1720	1943	1052	1692	1943
1049	1335	1939			

They were used chiefly in mail and newspaper trains, occasionally with passenger trains, and all lasted until the end of steam operation in the Island on 31st December, 1966.

Until 1939, passenger luggage vans were painted sage green with black ends and underframe and white roof. At least two vans were repainted grey, presumably because of a shortage of green paint both during and immediately after the War, these being No. 1265 in July 1942 and No. 1957 at Eastleigh in April 1946. Most vans at this time were painted malachite green, with the title 'Southern' instead of 'Southern Railway' being displayed. From 1949 all vans were repainted in British Railways crimson; No. 1082, for example, was outshopped in that livery in January 1951 and No. 1957, the grey van mentioned above, became crimson in October 1949.

From mid-1956, repaints were again in green, slightly darker than malachite, but many vans were withdrawn still in red. Examples of these are Nos. 1061, 2001 and 2005 (all withdrawn in 1962). No. 1062 received its green livery in February 1958, No. 1082 in April 1958, and the push-and-pull fitted vans Nos. 1996, 2002 and 2004 had been so-repainted before their withdrawal in 1962. Nos. 1058/68 were *still* in red when withdrawn in 1972!

From June 1966 BR blue, applied by airless spraying instead of being brushed on, was specified but it was many years before green disappeared. Whatever the livery, vans usually ran in service in filthy external condition.

Most of the ex-SEC vans were withdrawn from capital stock in 1947/8, the vast majority being converted for departmental use as staff and tool or stores vans. They were ideal for the purpose. A few others lingered in traffic until 1959, the remainder going in 1962, including the push-and-pull vans. These were directly replaced by five vans from the 1950 batch, Nos. 1621–5 being fitted with air control apparatus and allocated to the few South Western Division push-and-pull services remaining: Swanage, Lymington and Yeovil Town. On the withdrawal of these services the vans reverted to the general pool.

During the 1950s most of the 1934/6-built vans (Nos. 1154–1250 and 2181–2230) were withdrawn and converted into mess vans; this involved cutting a window in each end and in a few cases removing the lozenge-shaped chalking panels from the bodysides. The last survivors in capital stock were No. 1218, withdrawn August 1973 and purchased by the Stour Valley Railway in July 1975; and No. 1225, withdrawn 1976 and sold to the Kent & East Sussex Railway a year later.

To accommodate cyclists who wished to take their machines to the Continent by boat train, 14 vans were fitted in 1951 with hooks to carry bicycles and distinguished externally by a stencilled bicycle outline on the bodyside. Nos. 1055, 1103, 1208 and 1728 each had 60 hooks and Nos. 1057, 1113, 1175, 1282, 1293, 1305, 1314, 1317, 1454 and 1882 each had 24 hooks. Of these, No. 1317 was specially marked to work between Ashford and Cannon Street, but seven of the others had daily workings in boat trains. No. 1317 conveyed new bicycles, made by Normans of Ashford, destined for London.

The diagrams of cycle vans during summer 1957 and summer 1958 were:

1. 9.00 am Victoria to Folkestone Hbr and 2.25 pm return.
2. 10.00 am Victoria to Dover Marine and 7.10 pm return.
3. 11.00 am Victoria to Dover Marine and 2.30 pm return.
4. 1.30 pm Victoria to Folkestone Hbr and 8.50 pm return.
5. 2.30 pm Victoria to Dover Marine and 6.10 pm return.
6. 9.31 am Victoria to Newhaven Hbr and 6.15 pm return.
7. Spare at Victoria.
8. Spare at Dover Marine.
9. 6.09 am Newhaven Hbr to Victoria and 8.20 pm return.
10. Spare at Eardley.

In 1962 Nos. 1175 and 1208 were withdrawn and by 1966 No. 1317 had lost its 'Ashford–Cannon Street' designation. Cycle vans were no longer provided after 1969 and the vehicles reverted to the general pool.

One of the many PMVs converted to departmental vehicles and given a window in the end: No. 1192 (Ashford, June 1935), which was renumbered DS 90 about 1956 seen here at Three Bridges depot, 27th August, 1990. *Author*

PMV No. 1558 was given through connections for electric heating in 1961 and air brakes in 1967, but after only a few years was transferred to the Western Region where it became DB 975567 in the departmental list. Here shown in Roath Branch sidings, Cardiff, on 13th August, 1977, shortly before going for scrap to Woodhams, Barry. *Author*

In the 1950s the working of PMVs was still not very systematised and many parcels trains were formed of 'PMV as required'. This presupposed a huge fleet of vans occupying sidings at all the most important stations and which could be drawn on at a moment's notice. And no doubt it was so, until Dr Beeching came along and instructed that 'idle' vehicles must be eliminated. By 1963 every van working in traffic was given a separate working number, the formation of every parcels train was precisely laid down, and spare vehicles for maintenance were very few. That still left a good supply of parcels vans, as the traffic in mails and parcels was booming during the 1960s and 1970s.

An occasional use for spare vans in the 1950s was in hop-pickers' special trains, which were an annual event until the mechanisation of hop-picking. Each special would include several vans loaded with camping equipment, prams and chattels.

BR's redesignation of the passenger luggage vans as parcels and miscellaneous vans was fair enough as they were seldom used to carry passengers' accompanied luggage. It was only in boat trains that they continued this function until these trains were replaced by electric multiple units in June 1961. The 'Golden Arrow' remained, but was now electrically hauled. In October 1961 two vans, Nos. 1537 and 1558, were given through connections in order that the electric heating from locomotive through to the carriages could be maintained. These vans were then formed in the 'Golden Arrow' service; on the down journey the front van was for accompanied luggage and the rear van for registered luggage. They were replaced by BR-built general utility vans in July 1967.

On the Central Division too there was a need for electrically-wired PMVs, for steam traction on the Oxted and Reading–Tonbridge lines was almost finished. To work with electric-heated carriage stock Nos. 1499, 1626 and 1647 were converted in 1964 and Nos. 1455/76/82/95/96 in 1965/6. A further interesting development in 1967 was the conversion of these vans from vacuum to air brakes, because from 10th July, 1967 all remaining locomotive-hauled trains on the Oxted and Reading–Tonbridge lines were formed of air-braked stock and many of them included one or two vans for mails and parcels. The 10 vans fitted with air brakes and electric wiring (EWAB) were Nos. 1455/76/82/95/6/9, 1537/58, 1626/47. Workings of 'EWAB' vans, in 1967/8 until closure of the line between Lewes and Uckfield, were:

Working 484	SX	6.25 am Victoria to Brighton via Ashurst and 6.53 pm return.
	SO	6.25 am Victoria to Brighton via Ashurst and 9.53 am return.
Working 485	SX	5.20 am Victoria to East Croydon, 3.55 pm thence to East Grinstead and 8.31 pm to Victoria.
	SO	5.20 am Victoria to Brighton via Ashurst and 8.30 pm return.
Working 487 and 488 (two vans)	SX	6.49 am Reading to Redhill (MX), 6.41 pm to Tonbridge (MX), 7.46 pm Tonbridge to Reading.
	SO	6.49 am Reading to Redhill and 12.45 pm ety to Tonbridge. Attached to 7.46 pm following Monday.

Working 489   SX   4.40 pm Redhill to Reading, 11.24 pm Reading to
                          Guildford and 12.21 am vans and empty stock to
                          Redhill.
                     SO   7.46 am Redhill to Reading, then as Mondays to
                          Fridays.

The vans of the 7.46 pm from Tonbridge were loaded with parcel post, the front van conveying bags for Redhill and Guildford and the second van items for Reading and anything to be forwarded by the Western Region.

Keeping the air-braked vans to restricted circuits prevented any problems of mixed vacuum/air-braked operation of PMVs arising. But there was one exception. At Guildford three vacuum-braked vans, which had arrived from Woking, Aldershot and Portsmouth respectively, had to be attached to the rear of the 12.21 am service to Redhill, and the answer to the problem was to include a fitted goods brake van at the tail. The locomotive operated the air brakes on the three carriages and PMV, but could not operate the vacuum brakes of the vehicles behind, the necessary braking power being provided by the fitted goods brake van. This mixed-brake train continued running until May 1975, after the replacement by April 1973 of SR PMVs by BR general utility vans.

The 'EWAB' vans had a fairly short life. The Oxted line van workings ceased in January 1969, leaving only three PMVs in regular use on most of the Tonbridge–Reading locomotive-hauled trains until 1973. The 10 vans were transferred to the Western Region in June 1973, officially 'on loan', but they were never returned. In 1976/7 they were renumbered as departmental vehicles but three were condemned at once and a fourth by 1985. Six remained in 1990. No other vehicle of Southern Railway origin was ever converted to air braking after 1967.

Although the main use for PMVs was for carrying letters, parcels and newspapers, there was still in 1966 a very small amount of fish traffic. One interesting working of a PMV conveying fish was in the 4.50 am London Bridge to Dover van train. At Folkestone East the PMV was detached and worked down the steep Harbour branch by freight train. The fish that had been brought from London was destined for the Continent. During the day the van, having been emptied of its scaly contents, was loaded with mails from the Continent, next being worked back up to Folkestone East by the 5.00 pm freight train. It then formed part of a van train for Cannon Street leaving at 5.22 pm.

Southern PMVs could be seen almost anywhere in the country and one might be forgiven for thinking that the vans were 'common user', like wagons. However, examination of the working notices shows that such vans for the most part were on through workings from or to the Southern Region, which remained responsible for their maintenance. No doubt other Regions 'borrowed' Southern vans for days at a time, and perhaps the laid-down diagrams were not always adhered to, but sooner or later every van on a 'foreign' Region returned to the Southern.

In 1966, for example, a van train left Ramsgate at 5.55 pm Mondays to Fridays with PMVs for several destinations, reached via Reading. There was one for Cardiff, loaded with parcel post for Cardiff, Cheltenham, Gloucester,

Swindon and Newport; one for Leeds, loaded for Leeds, Bradford and Sheffield; one for Nottingham; one for Leicester, loaded for Derby and Leicester; and one for Birmingham, loaded for Birmingham, Oxford, Shrewsbury and Worcester. In 1967 an overnight van train left Brighton with PMVs for Birmingham, Nottingham, Edinburgh, Leeds, Cardiff and Bristol, again reached via Redhill and Reading.

By 1973 there were at least six of these van trains every night, all of which converged on Clapham Junction to be re-sorted into four trains which were forwarded via the West London line: two for London Midland Region destinations, one for Eastern Region and one for Western Region destinations. These were the trains:

8.05 pm from Margate	Forwarded from Clapham Jn at
1 PMV for York	3.15 am
1 PMV for Leeds	3.15 am
1 PMV for Nottingham	3.00 am
2 PMV for Birmingham	1.15 am
1 PMV for Oldham	1.15 am

8.40 pm from Dover Priory	Forwarded from Clapham Jn at
2 PMV for Rugby	1.15 am
1 PMV for Oldham	1.15 am
1 PMV for Glasgow	1.15 am
1 PMV for Birmingham	1.15 am
1 PMV for Nottingham	3.00 am
2 PMV for Leeds	3.15 am
1 PMV for York	3.15 am
1 PMV for Bristol	3.42 am

8.00 pm from Andover	Forwarded from Clapham Jn at
1 PMV for Rugby	1.15 am
1 PMV for York	3.15 am

10.39 pm from Guildford	Forwarded from Clapham Jn at
1 PMV for Cardiff	3.42 am
1 PMV for Bristol	3.42 am
2 PMV for York	3.15 am
1 PMV for Nottingham	3.00 am
2 PMV for Rugby	1.15 am

11.05 pm from Twickenham	Forwarded from Clapham Jn at
1 PMV for Bristol	3.42 am
1 PMV for Peterborough	3.15 am
1 PMV for Nottingham	3.00 am
1 PMV for Birmingham	1.15 am
1 PMV for Oldham	1.15 am
1 PMV for Manchester	1.15 am
1 PMV for Glasgow	1.15 am
3 PMV for Rugby	1.15 am

12.30 am from Redhill	Forwarded from Clapham Jn at
1 PMV for Rugby	3.00 am
1 PMV for Leeds	3.15 am
1 PMV for York	3.15 am

The three vans in the 12.30 am from Redhill had worked from Bricklayers Arms the previous morning to East Croydon, where they had stood all afternoon in the Post Office siding to be loaded. At 9.42 pm they had left for Redhill, where they were attached to a van train from Brighton to Clapham Junction. In later years these 'East Croydon vans' were reduced to two, loaded for Crewe and Leeds; the Crewe van now ran via Redhill and Reading but the Leeds van worked via Redhill and Clapham Junction as before. They were almost invariably Southern vans.

In the late 1960s and 1970s PMVs could be seen on the Kyle of Lochalsh line, probably the furthest from home they ever reached. A regular PMV working in Scotland was in the 6.55 am Perth to Inverness, the van having arrived from Manchester. Another 'regular' was the van in the 6.00 am Glasgow Queen Street to Fort William, observed in both 1968 and 1978. Also in 1978 a PMV was seen on the 4.42 am Perth to Inverness, and Perth attached another to the 4.40 pm Inverness to Edinburgh. Southern vans were no strangers to East Anglia, either; No. 1493 was at Cambridge on 24th July, 1969 and No. 2540 was there on 6th August, 1969, and on 5th August, 1975 a PMV was formed in the 10.23 am from Norwich to Lowestoft passenger train.

Occasionally when a Southern PMV turned up in another Region it might find itself being hauled by a diesel-mechanical multiple unit. As both unit and van were vacuum braked it was perfectly practicable, but as the diesels were somewhat underpowered it is thought that no more than one van at a time could be hauled. The Western, the Region that remained so endearingly different from the other parts of British Railways, was the chief specialist in the practice of hanging vans on to railcars, but it was not unheard-of elsewhere; for example, on 28th March, 1970 the 1.10 pm Grimsby to Peterborough dmu had a Southern PMV as tail-load.

In 1966 the following WR dmus working on to the Southern were booked to haul a PMV:

> 10.38 pm Basingstoke to Salisbury (SX), 7.15 pm Basingstoke to Salisbury (SO).
> 6.33 am and 11.05 pm Reading to Basingstoke.
> 5.45 am and 9.48 am Bristol to Weymouth.
> 7.35 pm Weymouth to Bristol.

By 1968 only the 6.00 and 9.40 am Bristol to Weymouth dmus were still hauling a PMV and by the early 1970s the practice had ceased. PMVs working on to the Western were now locomotive-hauled only. From 1975 to 1978 a van in the 1.50 am (Mondays excepted) from Eastleigh to Bristol was detached at Salisbury, later being attached to the coaches forming the 6.26 am to Exeter. Another PMV (or maybe the same one) was formed in the 4.00 pm Exeter to Barnstaple and 5.52 pm return – both locomotive-hauled passenger trains.

Withdrawals of the older vans continued steadily throughout the 1970s, but there were still a few hundred remaining when in June 1981, BR withdrew its Parcels Collection and Delivery service. At once there was a huge increase in the number of 'surplus' parcels vans and the result was a rapid withdrawal of the vast majority of former Company-owned vans. The last Southern-design PMV (No. 1865) was withdrawn in July 1986.

Of the vast number of SR passenger luggage vans that was built, it has to be said that a very large number has been acquired by the various private railways around the country. Some of the examples have been painted up nicely, but virtually all are used for storage of materials and do not usually run in passenger trains. Here is a list of all known PMVs in private ownership:

  153   (SEC number) To Bluebell Railway as DS 70031, 11.1973. Mess van.
1052   To Isle of Wight Steam Railway, Haven Street, 5.1976.
1070   To Conwy Valley Railway Museum, 8.1974.
1108   To Quainton Railway Preservation Society, 3.1973.
1119   To Kent & East Sussex Railway, 1977. Required for underframe only.
1125   To Keighley & Worth Valley Railway, 7.1973.
1137   To East Somerset Railway, 11.1973.
1145   To Kent & East Sussex Railway as DS 70217, 12.1984. PW mess & tool van.
1152   To Stour Valley Railway, 7.1975.
1153   To Great Central Railway, Loughborough, c.1986.
1184   To Bluebell Railway as KDS 164, 6.1986. S & T van.
1218   To Stour Valley Railway, 7.1975.
1225   To Kent & East Sussex Railway, 1977. Required for underframe only.
1227   To Dean Forest Railway, 1982.
1228   To Kent & East Sussex Railway as DS 800, 5.1990. Required for underframe.
1234   To Swanage Railway as DS 3065, 1977.
1248   To Kent & East Sussex Railway as DS 161, 2.1984. Body grounded at Rolvenden.
1304   To North Yorkshire Moors Railway, 1982.
1396   To East Somerset Railway, 11.1973.
1566   To Isle of Wight Steam Railway, 11.1981. Required for underframe only.
1617   To Isle of Wight Steam Railway, 8.1982. Required for underframe only.
1650   To East Somerset Railway, 7.1983.
1669   To Isle of Wight Steam Railway, c.11.1981. Required for underframe only.
1783   To Isle of Wight Steam Railway, 11.1981. Required for underframe only.
1788   To Bluebell Railway, 11.1981. Civil Engineers van.
1803   To Isle of Wight Steam Railway, 8.1982. Required for underframe only.
1808   To Kent & East Sussex Railway, 5.1981. Gangwayed one end to run with Pullman, 6.1984.
1851   To Mid-Hants Railway, 10.1976.
1855   Preserved at Bodmin Road Station, post-1983.
1865   To Midland Railway Centre, 12.1986. Required for underframe only.
1995   To Mid-Hants Railway as DS 792, 10.1976. Ex-SEC van.
2012   To Kent & East Sussex Railway as ADS 1035, 3.1990. Ex-SEC van.
2151   To North Yorkshire Moors Railway, 1982.
2186   To Bluebell Railway as KDS 150, 12.1979. Maunsell Locomotive Society mess van.
2188   To Mid-Hants Railway as DS 11, 3.1979.
2196   To Mid-Hants Railway as DS 93, 3.1976.

SR DIAGRAM No. 960

TARE 13 TONS (No. 1972, 12 TONS)

EX-SECR PASSENGER LUGGAGE VAN

SR NOS. 1972 – 2016.

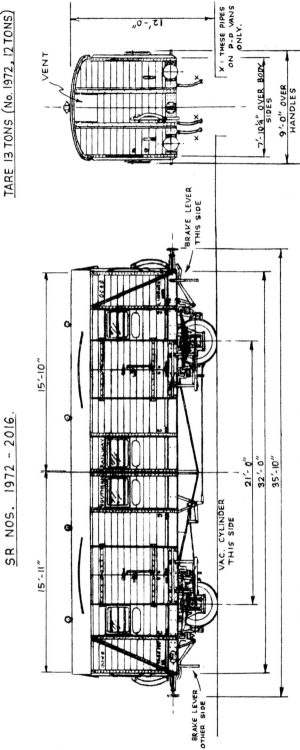

VENT

12'-0"

X : THESE PIPES ON P-P VANS ONLY.

7'-10¼" OVER BODY SIDES

9'-0" OVER HANDLES

BRAKE LEVER THIS SIDE

15'-10"

15'-11"

21'-0"

32'-0"

35'-10"

VAC. CYLINDER THIS SIDE

BRAKE LEVER OTHER SIDE

No. 1972 ONLY : NO CHALKING PANELS UNDER CENTRE LIGHTS

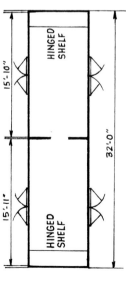

HINGED SHELF

HINGED SHELF

15'-10"

15'-11"

32'-0"

DRAWN BY M. S. KING

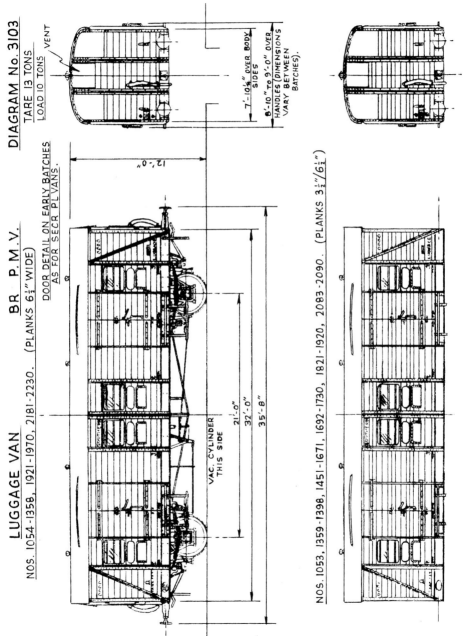

DIAGRAM No. 3103

BR P.M.V.

TARE 13 TONS
LOAD 10 TONS

LUGGAGE VAN

NOS. 1054-1358, 1921-1970, 2181-2230. (PLANKS 6½″ WIDE)

DOOR DETAIL ON EARLY BATCHES AS FOR SECR PL VANS.

VENT

7′-10½″ OVER BODY SIDES

8′-10″ TO 9′-0″ OVER HANDLES (DIMENSIONS VARY BETWEEN BATCHES).

12′-0″

VAC. CYLINDER THIS SIDE

21′-0″

32′-0″

35′-8″

NOS. 1053, 1359-1398, 1451-1671, 1692-1730, 1821-1920, 2083-2090. (PLANKS 3½″/6½″)

DRAWN BY M. S. KING

In 1942 Lancing constructed a batch of vans with unusual body strapping. Here is one of these vans at Ashford, showing the vertical steel plates to which are bolted lengths of timber. *M.S. King*

End of van No. 1788 (Lancing, 1942) showing the steel and timber strapping and vacuum brake pipe. This van was at West Hoathly on The Bluebell Railway seen on 7th April, 1991. *Author*

PMV No. 1794, built at Lancing in 1942, with body planking of equal-width planks except for the centre one, and the combined steel and timber strapping. Clapham Junction, 4th March, 1977. *Author*

SUMMARY OF SEC 32 FT LUGGAGE VANS

SR No.	Built	SEC No.	Re-No.	At	Remarks
1972	1919	132	11.25	Ashford	To 374S, 8.46. Re-no. 082757, 7.67.
3	1921	121	6.26	,,	To 788S, 1948. Withdrawn 1970.
4	,,	122	11.25	,,	To 745S, 1947. Withdrawn c.1975.
5	,,	123	3.26	,,	To 448S, 1947. Withdrawn 10.61.
6	,,	124	11.25	,,	To DS70023, 6.59. Withdrawn 3.70.
7	,,	125	7.26	,,	To 1026S, 1948. Withdrawn c.80.
8	,,	136	3.26	,,	To 474S, 1947. Withdrawn c.78.
9	,,	137	3.26	,,	To 859S, 1948. Withdrawn c.75.
1980	,,	138	7.26	,,	To 287S, 8.46. Withdrawn c.68.
1	,,	139	11.25	,,	To 3765S, 8.46. Re-no. 083237, 4.76.
2	,,	140	3.26	,,	Withdrawn ?
3	,,	141	6.26	,,	To 785S, 1948. Withdrawn 3.59.
4	,,	142	3.26	,,	To 367S, 1947. Withdrawn c.65.
5	,,	143	6.26	,,	To 218S, 3.46. Withdrawn c.74.
6	,,	144	6.26	,,	To 385S, 1946. Withdrawn c.72.
7	,,	145	7.26	,,	To 97S, 7.46. Re-no. 081033, 1958.
8	,,	146	7.26	,,	To 373S, 1946. Withdrawn c.75.
9	,,	147	3.26	,,	Withdrawn ?
1990	,,	148	7.26	,,	To 749S, 1948. Withdrawn c.75.
1	,,	149	7.26	,,	To 251S, 8.45. Withdrawn c.75.
2	,,	150	8.26	,,	Withdrawn ?
3	1922	152	10.28	,,	To 747S, 1947. Withdrawn c.84.
4	8.22	153	8.30	,,	To DS70031, 1959. Withdrawn 1973.
5	,,	154	6.29	,,	To DS792, 1949. Withdrawn 1976.
6	,,	155	5.29	,,	To DS70165, 12.62. Withdrawn c.89.
7	,,	157	6.29	,,	To 787S, 1948. Withdrawn 1977.
8	,,	158	5.29	,,	To 784S, 1948. Extant 1.90.
9	,,	160	6.29	,,	To 1099S, 1948. Withdrawn c.75.
2000	,,	161	7.29	,,	To 449S, 1947. Withdrawn c.75.
1	,,	162	7.27	,,	To DS70166, 12.62. Withdrawn 1989.
2	,,	163	3.28	Lancing	To DS70205, 1.64. Withdrawn 3.72.
3	,,	166	5.29	,,	To 790S, 1948. Withdrawn c.73.
4	,,	167	6.29	,,	To DS70204, 3.64. Withdrawn 3.76.
5	,,	168	6.29	,,	Withdrawn 12.62.
6	,,	169	7.29	,,	To 446S, 1947. Withdrawn c.72.
7	,,	170	6.29	,,	To 789S, 1948. Withdrawn 1971.
8	,,	172	8.29	,,	Withdrawn 6.43.
9	9.22	173	6.29	,,	To 282S, 5.39. Withdrawn 1970.
2010	,,	174	7.29	,,	To 751S, 1948. Withdrawn c.83.
1	1922	175	6.29	,,	To 744S, 1947. Withdrawn c.76.
2	,,	177	10.28	,,	To 1035S, 1948. Withdrawn c.88.
3	,,	179	7.29	,,	To 750S, 1948. Withdrawn 1970.
4	,,	180	1.30	Eastleigh	To 786S, 1948. Withdrawn c.75.
5	,,	181	6.29	Ashford	To 742S, 1947. Withdrawn c.78.
2016	,,	182	5.29	,,	To 743S, 1947. Withdrawn 1978.

4-WHEELED LUGGAGE VANS
Summary of Building and Withdrawal Dates

Built	Withdrawn	Built	Withdrawn
1053 1943	10.82	1094 8.36	3.72
4 11.36	11.76	5 8.36	7.72
5 12.36	6.72	6 2.37	77
6 12.36	8.43	7 10.36 To DS70287,	7.73
7 4.37	1.68	4.69	
8 4.36	8.72	8 10.36	5.68
9 12.36 To DB975124,	c.80	9 10.36	11.76
71		1100 7.36	12.66
1060 6.36	6.76	1 10.36	10.67
1 5.36 To 082200,		2 8.36	3.81
64		3 8.36 To DS70291,	4.71
2 5.36 To 082046,		12.69	
1.64		4 3.36 Wath	6.78
3 7.36	3.69	5 8.36 To DS70216,	12.70
4 4.36	c.10.80	10.64	
5 4.36	12.62	6 8.36	81
6 2.37 To DS70232,	9.78	7 7.36 To ADB975424,	
9.65		75	
7 10.36	2.68	8 7.36	3.72
8 10.36	8.72	9 7.36	9.66
9 11.36	c.7.69	1110 8.36	10.72
1070 10.36	2.73	1 8.36	5.66
1 10.36	by 3.81	2 8.36	11.43
2 1.37 To 748S,	c.75	3 7.36 Clapham Jn	7.78
12.47		4 10.36 Accident damage	6.66
3 10.36	12.42	5 9.36	2.73
4 12.36	c.5.81	6 9.36	8.71
5 12.36 To 081620,		7 12.36	8.71
11.62		8 2.37	3.81
6 3.36	12.62	9 10.36	76
7 3.36	4.67	1120 1.37 To 083268,	
8 3.36	c.12.75	5.78	
9 3.36	c.7.81	1 2.37	c.3.81
1080 10.36	3.69	2 11.36	12.62
1 12.36	5.73	3 1.37	79
2 12.36	5.67	4 10.36 To 083055,	c.89
3 11.36	1.73	11.72	
4 12.36	3.72	5 2.37	2.73
5 4.37	4.72	6 10.36	80
6 9.36 To Mobile	4.40	7 9.36	9.43
Workshop		8 7.36	10.78
7 10.36	8.82	9 6.36	12.62
8 9.36	7.72	1130 3.36	8.71
9 9.36	6.78	1 2.37	12.71
1090 1.37	c.7.81	2 2.37	6.71
1 9.36	2.73	3 3.36	4.68
2 8.36	10.67	4 3.36 To IOW No.	12.66
3 8.36	8.71	1046	

Built		Withdrawn	Built		Withdrawn
1135	6.36	12.62	1166	5.35 To DS3157,	
6	6.36	12.71		50	
7	6.36	12.71		Re-no. 083037,	
8	6.36	11.72		7.72	
9	3.36	7.72	7	5.35 To DS159,	c.80
1140	6.36	11.76		2.57	
1	6.36	12.72	8	5.35 To DS8,	77
2	5.36 To DS70230,	c.89		53	
	65		9	8.35 To DS153,	
3	5.36	76		11.56	
4	4.36	c.10.81		Re-no. 083392,	
5	5.36 To DS70217,	c.83		3.80	
	2.66		1170	8.35 To DS91	c.72
6	5.36	10.72		2.56	
7	5.36	12.62	1	8.35 To DS29,	c.75
8	4.36 To 083146,			2.55	
	5.73		2	8.35 To DS798,	
9	4.36 Doncaster	9.80		50	
1150	5.36 To DS70314,	3.72	3	8.35 To DS3080,	c.75
	4.70			49	
1	5.36	1.68	4	8.35 To DS70004,	c.89
2	1.37	9.73		59	
3	1.37	12.85	5	8.35	12.62
4	4.35 To DS70139,	c.83	6	8.35 To DS70056,	89
	8.61			59	
5	4.35 To DS3175,	c.83	7	7.35 To DS70074,	c.89
	6.50			2.60	
6	4.35 To DS156,		8	7.35 To DS1538,	c.75
	12.56			49	
7	6.35 To DS3176,	c.70	9	7.35 To DS806,	77
	50			7.50	
8	6.35 To DS1715,	c.75	1180	8.35 To DS809,	c.75
	49			9.50	
9	5.35 To DS158,	c.82	1	8.35 To DS3066,	c.73
	1.57			50	
1160	5.35 To DS165,		2	8.35	12.62
	2.58		3	6.35 To DS168,	c.75
1	4.35 To DS1539,	c.75		5.57	
	49		4	6.35 To DS164,	
2	5.35 To DS149,			12.57	
	8.54		5	7.35 To DS3063,	c.75
3	5.35 To DS7,	72		50	
	53		6	6.35 To DS5,	77
4	4.35 To DS808,	c.75		53	
	7.50		7	6.35 To DS3,	4.82
5	6.35	11.43		53	

Built	Withdrawn	Built	Withdrawn
1188 6.35	9.43	1212 12.35 To DS1103,	
9 6.35 To DS4,	89	6.49	
53		Re-no. 083185,	
1190 6.35 To DS1102,		3.75	
49		3 12.35 To DS70006,	89
Re-no. 083352,		58	
9.78		4 12.35 To DS802,	8.71
1 6.35 To DS811,	c.82	6.50	
50		5 12.35 To DS31,	
2 6.35 To DS90,		2.55	
2.56		6 12.35 To DS167,	
3 7.35 To DS166,		5.57	
5.57		7 2.36	12.62
4 7.35 To DS70043,	6.72	8 2.36	8.73
11.59		9 2.36 To DS805,	c.75
5 7.35 Mobile workshop	12.42	7.50	
6 7.35	12.41	1220 2.36	11.72
7 7.35 To DS148	6.82	1 2.36	c.78
8.54		2 1.36 To DB975125,	
8 6.35 To DS793,	72	c.71	
49		3 1.36 To DS3062,	
9 6.35 To DS70032,	76	1.50	
11.59		Re-no. 083351,	
1200 6.35 Mobile workshop	c.40	9.78	
1 8.35 To 281S,		4 1.36 To DS795,	c.85
6.39		2.50	
Re-no. 1201,		5 1.36	76
N.D.		6 1.36	4.67
2 5.35 To DS791,	c.83	7 1.36 Cardiff	1.81
5.49		8 10.35 To DS800,	c.89
3 5.35 To DS70021,	2.78	50	
12.58		9 10.35 To DS3156,	c.80
4 11.35 To DS70005,	c.83	4.50	
8.58		1230 9.35	11.43
5 11.35 To DS801,	c.89	1 9.35 To DS171,	c.75
6.50		12.57	
6 11.35 To DS157,		2 9.35 To DS145,	c.75
1.57		6.54	
7 12.35 To DS797,	c.75	3 9.35 To DS143,	
3.50		3.54	
8 9.35 To DS70223,	10.77	4 9.35 To DS3065,	6.76
12.64		50	
9 9.35 To DS2,	c.89	5 9.35 To DS13,	
53		2.54	
1210 11.35 To DS796,	10.83	6 10.35 To DS6,	
2.50		11.53	
1 11.35 To DS146,	c.89	Re-no. 083410,	
6.54		11.81	

Built	Withdrawn	Built	Withdrawn
1237 9.35 To DS803, 6.50	3.77	1269 5.39	c.8.81
8 10.35 To DS3158, 4.50	c.75	1270 5.39	10.81
9 10.35	12.43	1 5.39 Margam	3.81
1240 10.35 To DS154, 11.56	c.1.90	2 5.39	c.7.81
1 10.35 To DS3061, 49	7.78	3 4.39	11.66
2 10.35 To DS163, 7.57 Re-no. 083428, 11.81		4 4.39 Hexthorpe	10.78
		5 2.39	10.66
3 11.35 To DS10, 1.54	6.76	6 3.39	2.82
4 11.35 To DS162, 7.57	c.78	7 4.39 Doncaster	c.3.81
5 11.35 To DS144, 4.54	c.89	8 7.39	c.11.81
6 10.35 To DS807, 7.50	c.89	9 3.39	c.10.81
7 11.35 To DS117, 12.57	77	1280 3.39	c.5.81
8 12.35 To DS161, 7.57	4.82	1 3.39	c.11.81
9 12.35 To DS160, 4.57		2 4.39 Severn Tunnel Jn	4.82
1250 12.35 To DS804, 7.50	3.77	3 4.39 To IOW No. 1047	12.66
1 2.39	12.41	4 5.39	c.5.81
2 2.39 Hexthorpe	10.78	5 3.39	81
3 2.39	c.4.81	6 3.39	c.7.81
4 2.39	c.11.81	7 5.39	c.5.81
5 6.39	c.4.81	8 5.39	c.10.81
6 3.39	2.82	9 5.39	c.5.81
7 3.39	9.83	1290 3.39	c.3.81
8 4.39 Selhurst	1.81	1 6.39 To 024670, 11.85	
9 4.39 Doncaster	5.78	2 3.39	10.68
1260 4.39	by 3.81	3 6.39	2.82
1 8.39	6.82	4 3.39	c.4.81
2 4.39 Hexthorpe	10.78	5 3.39	c.10.81
3 3.39	1.83	6 4.39	c.7.81
4 4.39	c.10.81	7 4.39	10.82
5 2.39 Damaged Clapham Jn	3.71	8 4.39 Bricklayers Arms	5.81
		9 6.39 Penzance	10.76
6 2.39	c.8.81	1300 3.39	12.43
7 3.39	10.82	1 5.39	c.10.81
8 5.39	by 3.81	2 5.39	c.2.81
		3 6.39	10.82
		4 5.39	c.8.81
		5 3.39	c.4.81
		6 3.39	by 8.78
		7 5.39	c.6.81
		8 5.39	c.11.81
		9 6.39	c.7.81
		1310 5.39	c.8.81
		1 5.39	7.82
		2 5.39 Sold to W.D. Long Marston	c.41

Built	Withdrawn	Built	Withdrawn
1313 5.39 To 041682, 3.84		1356 7.39	4.82
4 6.39	c.9.81	7 6.39 Margam	3.81
5 7.39	c.5.81	8 6.39	c.3.81
6 7.39 Bricklayers Arms	5.81	9 7.39 To DS70283, 69	
7 10.39	c.4.81	1360 10.39	2.83
8 8.39 Bricklayers Arms	5.81	1 10.39	c.4.81
9 7.39	c.6.81	2 10.39 Damaged W.Ealing	8.72
1320 7.39	by 3.81	3 10.39	81
1 7.39 To IOW, No. 1050	12.66	4 11.39 Bricklayers Arms	5.81
2 7.39	c.10.80	5 11.39 Bricklayers Arms	5.81
3 7.39 To ADB975960, 80	c.89	6 10.39	81
4 6.39	by 3.81	7 10.39	81
5 6.39 Margam	3.81	8 10.39 To 024671, 11.85	
6 6.39	c.11.80	9 10.39	10.82
7 10.39 Margam	3.81	1370 10.39 To 041503, 7.80	c.89
8 10.39	2.82	1 9.39 Bricklayers Arms	5.81
9 10.39	5.82	2 10.39	c.7.81
1330 10.39	c.12.80	3 10.39	c.10.81
1 8.39 Margam	3.81	4 9.39	c.7.81
2 8.39 Bricklayers Arms	5.81	5 10.39 Doncaster	5.78
3 9.39	6.81	6 10.39 Bricklayers Arms	5.81
4 8.39 Doncaster	10.78	7 10.39	10.82
5 8.39 To IOW, No. 1049	12.66	8 10.39 Margam	3.81
6 8.39	c.7.81	9 11.39	c.3.81
7 7.39	12.40	1380 11.39 Damaged	9.73
8 8.39	7.82	1 12.39	c.7.81
9 8.39	c.4.81	2 12.39	by 8.78
1340 8.39	post 80	3 12.39	c.3.81
1 8.39	c.11.81	4 12.39 To IOW, No. 1051	12.66
2 6.39	7.82	5 11.39	11.66
3 6.39	c.8.81	6 11.39 Damaged	12.73
4 6.39	c.3.81	7 11.39	c.11.81
5 6.39	c.3.81	8 12.39 Stonebridge Park	5.81
6 7.39	9.72	9 12.39	81
7 7.39	5.82	1390 12.39 Ipswich	10.81
8 7.39	post 80	1 11.39 Hexthorpe	6.78
9 9.39	1.82	2 11.39 Margam	3.81
1350 9.39 To DS1385, 5.49		3 10.39 Damaged Steven-age. Broken up on site	5.71
1 10.39	c.3.81	4 11.39	c.6.81
2 10.39	3.82	5 11.39	c.4.81
3 9.39 Doncaster	9.80	6 12.39	8.71
4 7.39	10.82		
5 7.39	c.11.81		

Built	Withdrawn	Built	Withdrawn
1397 12.39	c.8.81	1491 6.51	by 3.81
8 12.39	c.10.81	2 6.51 Stonebridge Park	5.81
1451 1.51	5.82	3 6.51	7.82
2 1.51	c.3.81	4 7.51	81
3 2.51	5.82	5 7.51 To DB975670,	
4 2.51	c.10.81	78	
5 2.51 To DB975669,		6 7.51 To DB975566,	
78		76	
6 2.51	c.11.81	7 8.51	81
7 2.51	c.9.81	8 8.51	by 5.71
8 2.51 Margam	3.81	9 8.51 To DB975569,	c.80
9 2.51	3.81	77	
1460 2.51 Eastleigh	4.78	1500 8.51	12.83
1 2.51 Barry	3.81	1 8.47	10.82
2 3.51	10.82	2 6.47	c.5.81
3 3.51 Doncaster	6.78	3 6.47	c.8.81
4 3.51	1.83	4 7.47	c.2.81
5 3.51	c.8.81	5 7.47 Cardiff	1.81
6 3.51 Barry	3.81	6 6.47	3.82
7 4.51	7.83	7 7.47 To ADB977182,	
8 4.51	c.12.80	83	
9 4.51 Whittlesea	3.81	8 7.47	12.82
1470 4.51	c.8.81	9 7.47	2.82
1 4.51 Damaged Camden	8.74	1510 7.47 Margam	3.81
2 5.51	c.10.81	1 8.47 Bricklayers Arms	5.81
3 5.51 Upperby	6.81	2 8.47	c.8.81
4 5.51	10.82	3 8.47	by 3.81
5 5.51	by 5.73	4 7.47 Margam	3.81
6 5.51 To DB975563,		5 7.47	c.8.81
76		6 7.47	c.3.81
7 5.51 Margam	3.81	7 7.47	c.8.81
8 5.51 To 024465,	c.89	8 7.47	6.82
9.82		9 7.47	10.82
9 5.51	6.82	1520 7.47	10.82
1480 6.51 Bricklayers Arms	5.81	1 7.47	c.8.81
1 6.51 Margam	3.81	2 6.47	c.5.81
2 6.51 To DB975564,	84	3 7.47	c.7.81
76		4 7.47	c.11.81
3 6.51	c.8.81	5 8.47	c.11.81
4 6.51	c.5.81	6 7.47	c.12.80
5 6.51	12.83	7 7.47	c.10.80
6 6.51 Mishap,	11.77	8 7.47	10.82
Paddington		9 8.47	c.9.81
7 6.51 Severn Tunnel Jn	4.82	1530 7.47	c.4.81
8 6.51 To 041678,		1 7.47	10.82
11.83		2 7.47	c.3.81
9 6.51	c.11.80	3 7.47	6.82
1490 6.51	c.3.81	4 8.47	by 3.81

Built	Withdrawn	Built	Withdrawn
1535 7.47	79	1577 1950	c.8.81
6 7.47 To ADB977183, 83		8 1950 Bricklayers Arms	5.81
7 8.47 To DB975570, 76	c.80	9 1950	c.11.81
8 8.47	10.82	1580 1950	8.82
9 8.47	c.9.81	1 12.50	by 5.75
1540 8.47 Margam	3.81	2 12.50	81
1 8.47 Margam	3.81	3 12.50	c.3.81
2 8.47	2.82	4 1950	81
3 8.47	81	5 1950	c.6.81
4 8.47	10.82	6 1950	10.82
5 8.47 Margam	3.81	7 1950 Margam	3.81
6 8.47	by 3.81	8 1950	c.11.81
7 7.47	c.3.81	9 1950	by 5.73
8 8.47	10.82	1590 1950 Bricklayers Arms	5.81
9 8.47	c.8.81	1 1950 To ADB977117, 82	
1550 8.47	c.8.81	2 1950	c.4.81
1 8.47	c.3.81	3 1950 Barry	3.81
2 8.47	c.5.81	4 1950 Craigentinny	6.81
3 7.47	c.5.81	5 1950	6.82
4 8.47	c.3.81	6 1950	c.10.81
5 8.47	c.10.81	7 1950 Stonebridge Park	5.81
6 8.47	c.5.81	8 1950	c.4.81
7 8.47	10.82	9 1950 Mishap, Euston	6.81
8 8.47 To DB975567, 76	c.78	1600 1950	5.82
9 7.47 Bricklayers Arms	5.81	1 1950	10.82
1560 7.47	c.7.81	2 1950	c.11.81
1 1950 To 083528, 4.84	c.89	3 1950	81
2 1950 To ADB975997, 80		4 1950	10.82
3 1950	2.82	5 1950 Old Oak	2.81
4 1950	c.5.81	6 1950	c.5.81
5 1950	c.7.81	7 1950	81
6 1950	c.8.81	8 1950	10.82
7 1950	6.82	9 12.50	10.82
8 1950 Margam	3.81	1610 12.50	81
9 1950	c.9.81	1 12.50	c.12.80
1570 12.50 Bricklayers Arms	5.81	2 1950 Margam	3.81
1 12.50	c.8.81	3 1950 Micheldever	9.78
2 1950	81	4 1950	c.7.81
3 12.50	c.11.81	5 1950 Margam	3.81
4 1950	c.3.81	6 1950	6.82
5 1950	c.8.81	7 1950	5.82
6 1950 To 083285, 7.80		8 1950 To 083433, 12.81	
		9 1950	c.8.81
		1620 12.50	c.5.81
		1 12.50	1.82
		2 12.50	c.10.81

Built	Withdrawn	Built	Withdrawn
1623 1950	c.10.80	1665 1950	c.8.81
4 12.50	12.83	6 1950	c.5.81
5 12.50	c.5.81	7 1950	by 3.81
6 1950 To DB975568, 76		8 1950	12.69
7 1950 Damaged Camden	10.74	9 1950	c.11.81
8 1950 To 083394, 7.80		1670 1950 Margam	3.81
9 1950 To ADB977045, 81	c.89	1 1950	c.4.81
1630 1950	7.77	1692 8.43 To IOW, No. 1052	12.66
1 1950 Doncaster	3.81	3 8.43	c.3.81
2 1950	c.3.81	4 8.43	81
3 1950	6.83	5 9.43	6.82
4 1950	3.82	6 9.43	c.11.81
5 1950	c.12.80	7 8.43	by 5.74
6 1950	6.82	8 8.43 Margam	3.81
7 1950 Margam	3.81	9 8.43 Margam	3.81
8 1950	10.82	1700 8.43	81
9 1950	c.4.82	1 9.43 Margam	3.81
1640 1950	c.3.81	2 5.43	c.12.80
1 1950	83	3 7.43	c.5.81
2 1950	c.78	4 5.43	c.6.80
3 1950	c.3.81	5 5.43	c.4.81
4 1950	11.85	6 5.43	4.82
5 1950	10.82	7 6.43	11.71
6 1950	c.8.81	8 6.43	c.78
7 1950 To DB975565, 76		9 6.43	10.82
8 1950	81	1710 6.43	81
9 1950	81	1 7.43	c.6.80
1650 1950	7.83	2 7.43	2.86
1 1950 Bricklayers Arms	5.81	3 7.43	5.82
2 1950	12.71	4 6.43	c.11.81
3 12.50	81	5 6.43	10.82
4 1950	81	6 6.43 Bricklayers Arms	5.81
5 1950 To 083471, 12.82		7 6.43	6.82
6 1950	1.68	8 6.43	10.82
7 1950 Broken up, Selhurst	3.77	9 6.43	c.11.81
8 1950 Broken up	8.84	1720 6.43 To IOW, No. 1048	12.66
9 1950 Broken up	8.84	1 6.43	c.8.81
1660 1950	c.11.81	2 7.43	3.81
1 1950	c.11.81	3 7.43	c.8.81
2 1950 Stonebridge Park	5.81	4 7.43 Hexthorpe	9.78
3 1950	81	5 7.43 Upperby	6.81
4 1950	12.82	6 7.43	6.82
		7 7.43	c.8.81
		8 7.43 To ADB977038, 10.81	
		9 7.43	c.3.81

Built		Withdrawn	Built		Withdrawn
1730	7.43	c.10.81	1826	3.40	c.10.81
1781	1942	10.82	7	2.40	81
2	1942	c.7.81	8	3.40	c.5.81
3	1942	c.8.81	9	3.40	c.8.81
4	1942	10.82	1830	2.40	8.82
5	11.42	9.73	1	2.40	c.9.77
6	1942	c.8.81	2	3.40	5.82
7	1942 To 466S,	c.75	3	3.40	c.8.81
	5.47		4	3.40 To 024536,	9.85
8	1942	c.8.81			
9	1942	c.7.81	5	3.40	10.82
1790	1942 Margam	3.81	6	3.40	c.7.81
1	1942 To 469S,	c.75	7	3.40 Margam	3.81
	5.47		8	3.40	c.12.80
2	1942	6.82	9	3.40	c.12.80
3	1942	10.82	1840	3.40	3.71
4	1942	c.5.81	1	3.40	c.8.81
5	1942	c.8.81	2	3.40 Hexthorpe	9.78
6	1942	c.6.81	3	3.40	10.82
7	1942	10.82	4	3.40 Margam	3.81
8	1942	c.11.81	5	3.40	c.3.81
9	1942	6.82	6	3.40	c.11.81
1800	1942 Hexthorpe	6.78	7	3.40	c.10.80
1	1942	10.82	8	3.40	c.6.81
2	1942	5.82	9	3.40 Margam	3.81
3	1942	3.82	1850	3.40	c.1.82
4	1942	10.82	1	4.40	76
5	1942 Bricklayers Arms	5.81	2	3.40	c.8.81
6	1942	2.82	3	4.40	10.82
7	1942	c.81	4	4.40 To 083469,	12.82
8	1942	1.80			
9	1942	c.11.81	5	4.40	7.83
1810	1942	10.84	6	4.40	11.82
1	1942	10.82	7	4.40	c.3.81
2	1942	c.10.81	8	3.40 Margam	3.81
3	1942	10.82	9	4.40	c.11.81
4	1942	c.10.81	1860	4.40	by 3.81
5	1942	c.10.81	1	4.40 Bricklayers Arms	5.81
6	1942	8.82	2	4.40	7.82
7	1942	c.8.81	3	5.40	c.8.81
8	1942	10.82	4	4.40	c.2.81
9	1942	8.82	5	4.40	7.86
1820	1942	by 3.81	6	4.40	c.10.81
1	2.40	c.11.81	7	4.40	7.82
2	2.40	by 3.81	8	4.40 Margam	3.81
3	2.40	c.8.81	9	5.40	c.5.81
4	2.40	10.66	1870	4.40	7.69
5	2.40	10.82	1	6.40	c.10.81

Built	Withdrawn	Built	Withdrawn
1872 5.40	c.11.81	1916 8.40	11.82
3 4.40	c.4.81	7 8.40	12.82
4 4.40	10.82	8 5.40	c.11.81
5 5.40	c.12.80	9 5.40 Mishap, Exeter	8.61
6 5.40 Margam	3.81	1920 5.40	by 3.81
7 5.40	10.82	1 11.38	81
8 5.40 Margam	3.81	2 11.38	7.82
9 4.40	by 3.81	3 11.38	c.5.81
1880 4.40	c.11.81	4 11.38	c.8.81
1 4.40	c.3.81	5 11.38	8.82
2 4.40	c.11.81	6 11.38 Bricklayers Arms	5.81
3 4.40	c.2.81	7 10.38 Damaged beyond repair, Sheffield	1.60
4 4.40 Bricklayers Arms	5.81		
5 4.40	c.8.81	8 10.38	9.70
6 4.40 Upperby	6.81	9 11.38	11.66
7 4.40	c.10.81	1930 10.38	5.82
8 4.40 Hexthorpe	6.78	1 10.38 Stonebridge Park	5.81
9 4.40 Damaged Glasgow Queen Street. Broken up on site.	8.75	2 10.38	12.82
		3 10.38	12.82
		4 10.38	c.5.81
1890 4.40	c.3.81	5 10.38 Margam	3.81
1 4.40 Bricklayers Arms	5.81	6 10.38	c.5.81
2 4.40	c.4.81	7 11.38	c.3.81
3 5.40	c.5.81	8 12.38 To DB975277, c.73	c.89
4 5.40	c.4.81		
5 4.40	2.82	9 12.38	3.69
6 5.40	6.82	1940 12.38 Margam	3.81
7 5.40 To 024515, 5.84	c.89	1 12.38	3.81
		2 12.38	10.82
8 5.40 Margam	3.81	3 12.38	10.82
9 5.40	81	4 11.38 Accident damage, Manchester Victoria	4.67
1900 4.40	c.5.81		
1 5.40	81		
2 5.40	c.3.81	5 12.38	c.74
3 5.40	c.8.81	6 10.38	11.71
4 5.40	3.82	7 11.38 Margam	3.81
5 5.40	c.9.81	8 10.38 Mobile Workshop	12.42
6 5.40	81	9 11.38	4.82
7 5.40	81	1950 11.38 Doncaster	6.78
8 8.40	c.10.81	1 11.38	c.10.81
9 6.40	10.82	2 11.38	c.10.81
1910 8.40 Margam	3.81	3 10.38	81
1 6.40	c.10.80	4 11.38	c.11.81
2 6.40	c.4.81	5 11.38	c.8.81
3 5.40	c.5.81	6 12.38	c.5.81
4 5.40	10.82	7 11.38	10.72
5 8.40	c.10.81	8 11.38 Hexthorpe	6.78

Built	Withdrawn	Built	Withdrawn
1959 11.38 Fire damage	12.64	2116 9.42	c.8.81
1960 11.38	by 3.81	7 9.42	c.8.81
1 12.38	c.3.81	8 9.42	6.82
2 11.38	c.8.81	9 9.42	c.8.81
3 11.38	c.5.81	2120 9.42	76
4 11.38	6.83	1 9.42	10.82
5 12.38 Accident damage, Woking	4.73	2 9.42	c.3.81
		3 9.42 Margam	3.81
6 12.38	10.82	4 9.42	12.83
7 12.38	10.82	5 9.42 To 041551, 4.81	
8 11.38	c.9.81		
9 11.38 Doncaster	6.78	6 9.42	c.8.81
1970 11.38	3.66	7 9.42 To 470S, 5.47	77
2083 8.43	c.8.81		
4 7.43	c.5.81	8 9.42 Damaged W. Ealing	8.72
5 7.43	12.82		
6 7.43	10.82	9 9.42 To DB975962, 80	
7 8.43 Doncaster	6.78		
8 8.43	8.82	2130 9.42 Doncaster	6.78
9 8.43	c.10.81	1 9.42	c.11.81
2090 7.43	1.68	2 9.42	81
1 8.42	3.82	3 12.42	c.5.81
2 8.42	c.5.81	4 10.42	c.8.81
3 8.42	76	5 10.42	c.4.81
4 8.42 Damaged Oxheys	1.70	6 11.42	c.5.81
5 8.42 Upperby	6.81	7 11.42	1.82
6 8.42	81	8 11.42 To DS147, 8.54 Re-no. 083240, 10.76	c.89
7 8.42 To 083470, 12.82			
8 8.42 Damaged Bounds Green	6.60		
		9 11.42 Bricklayers Arms	5.81
9 9.42 Bricklayers Arms	5.81	2140 11.42	10.82
2100 9.42	10.82	1 9.42 Margam	3.81
1 9.42	10.82	2 9.42	c.6.82
2 9.42	c.4.81	3 10.42	c.11.81
3 8.42	10.82	4 11.42	c.4.81
4 8.42 Hexthorpe	6.78	5 11.42	10.82
5 8.42 Margam	3.81	6 10.42	post 1.81
6 8.42	81	7 10.42	10.82
7 9.42	c.7.81	8 10.42 Margam	3.81
8 9.42	by 3.81	9 11.42	c.8.81
9 9.42	c.10.81	2150 11.42	by 3.81
2110 9.42	10.82	1 12.42	c.8.81
1 9.42	c.11.81	2 12.42	5.82
2 9.42 Margam	3.81	3 12.42	1.78
3 9.42	c.7.81	4 12.42	3.81
4 9.42 Doncaster	6.81	5 12.42	c.9.81
5 9.42	c.7.81	6 12.42	12.82

Built	Withdrawn	Built	Withdrawn
2157 12.42	81	2197 12.34 To DS9,	
8 11.42	c.8.81	53	
9 11.42	c.75	Re-no. 083436,	
2160 11.42 Bricklayers Arms	5.81	c.82	
1 11.42	c.10.81	8 12.34	12.42
2 10.42	c.5.81	9 12.34 To DS139,	c.74
3 12.42 Bricklayers Arms	5.81	54	
4 12.42 To 471S,	c.75	2200 11.34 To DS152,	
5.47		10.56	
5 12.42	79	Re-no. 083287,	
6 12.42	10.82	10.77	
7 12.42 Severn Tunnel Jn	4.82	1 11.34	10.54
8 12.42	c.11.81	2 12.34 To DS169,	
9 12.42	10.82	12.57	
2170 12.42 Bricklayers Arms	5.81	3 12.34	10.54
2181 11.34 To DS36,		4 12.34 To DS155,	7.78
56		11.56	
2 11.34 To DS151.	89	5 12.34 To DS12,	
8.56		54	
3 10.34 To DS102,		Re-no. 083435,	
7.56.		3.82	
Re-no. 083350,		6 1.35 To DS70218,	
9.78		64	
4 10.34 To DS140,	72	7 1.35 To DS70059,	89
54		1.60	
5 11.34 To DS141,	71	8 1.35 To DS70020,	89
54		59	
6 12.34 To DS150,	c.7.78	9 1.35 To DS70018,	3.81
8.56		11.58	
7 11.34 To DS794,	70	2210 1.35 To DS3064,	
50		50	
8 11.34 To DS11,	c.7.78	Re-no. 083437,	
54		3.82	
9 12.34 To DS92,	c.76	1 1.35	8.41
7.56		2 3.35 To DS70055,	
2190 12.34	12.42	59	
1 11.34 To DS101,		3 3.35 To DS70154,	89
7.56		61	
2 11.34	8.43	4 3.35 To DS70022,	12.73
3 11.34 To DS138,	c.75	1.59	
54		5 1.35 To DS70144,	10.71
4 11.34 To DS70038,	7.71	12.61	
10.59		6 1.35 To DS70140,	4.80
5 11.34 To DS142,	72	61	
54		7 1.35 To DS70084,	7.76
6 12.34 To DS93,	c.75	9.60	
9.56			

Built		Withdrawn	Built		Withdrawn
2218	3.35 To DS70075, 5.60	4.81	2224	2.35	12.62
9	2.35 To DS70142, 6.61	11.71	5	3.35 To DS70156, 11.62	89
2220	2.35 To DS70148, 61	5.82	6	3.35	12.62
1	3.35	7.41	7	3.35 To DS810, 50	
2	3.35 Underframe to DS70174, 12.62	c.83	8	3.35 To DS70037, 59	
3	2.35 To DS70025, 59 Re-no. 041614, 9.82		9	2.35 To DS70215, 8.64	11.71
			2230	3.35 To DS70145, 11.61	12.81

Notes

1075 (081620) renumbered DS 70233, 1.65. Withdrawn c.83 and body grounded at Three Bridges depot.
DS70139 renumbered 083475, 6.83. Withdrawn c.89.
1562/76 converted to security vans for bullion, 11.63. Diagram 3104.
1613/18/28 converted to security vans for bullion, 11.63. Diagram 3104.
1201 renumbered DS 170, 12.57. Withdrawn c.75.

A much-renumbered 4-wheeled passenger luggage van at Selhurst Depot on 18th June, 1978. Originally SE&C No. 139, built by the Bristol Carriage & Wagon Co. in 1921, it became SR No. 1921 in 1925. In 1946 it was transferred to the service vehicles list as 375 S, and became an 'internal user' vehicle, No. 083237, in 1976.

Author

Chapter Five
Plastic-Bodied Luggage Vans

In 1944 ten 10-ton passenger luggage vans were built to test the suitability of plastic for railway vehicle construction. The outside panels and roof were constructed of reinforced plastic and, compared with the standard luggage vans, the weight was reduced by 2 tons 16 hundredweight and capacity increased by 40 cubic feet.

Length over headstocks was 33 ft, length over body 32 ft 2⅝ in., width over lock handles 8 ft 8⅞ in., width over body 8 ft 2½ in. and height from rail to roof was 12 ft 4¹⁵⁄₁₆ in. Wheelbase was 22 ft. Tare weight amounted to 10 tons 4 cwt. and the vans could load up to 10 tons distributed. The Diagram number was 3105 and the vehicle numbers were 1401–10 (Order No. 1659A).

The underframe was even more unusual than the body, for it incorporated a spring-cushioning device whose function was to relieve the underframe of inertia forces experienced by rigidly-fitted bodies – the reason why railway vehicles have to be strongly built. The body on each of these new vans was able to slide several inches longitudinally over the underframe against the resistance of the spring-cushioning device. It was only because of the spring-cushioning that it was possible to build both body and underframe of lighter materials than normal.

Rigidity and the ability to resist buffing shocks was provided by two girders running from end to end between the buffer planks, and independently sprung drawhooks were provided. Lifting of the body from the underframe was prevented by inwardly-facing clips attached two a side

Spring-cushioned, plastic-bodied luggage van No. 1409, built in August 1944. This official photograph of the van seems to have been taken after the van had been in traffic for some while, judging by the weathered appearance of the body and the chalk-marks on the solebar. *Courtesy National Railway Museum*

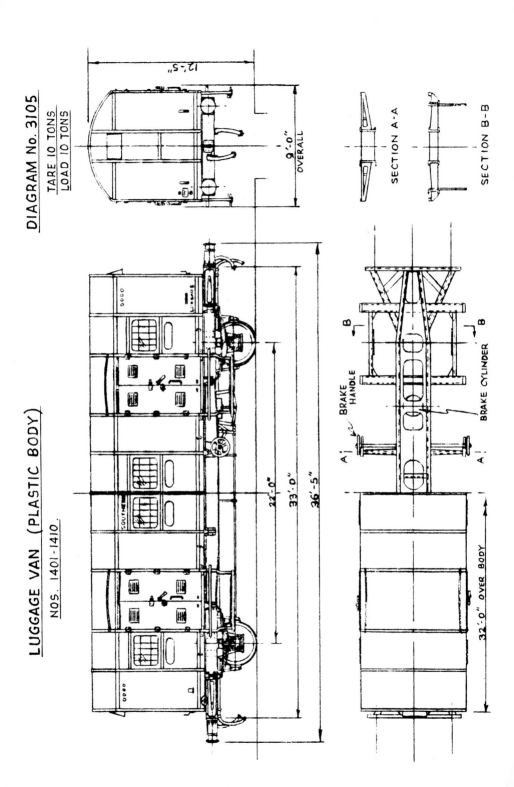

LUGGAGE VAN (PLASTIC BODY)

NOS. 1401–1410.

DIAGRAM No. 3105

TARE 10 TONS
LOAD 10 TONS

12'-5"

9'-0" OVERALL

SECTION A-A

SECTION B-B

22'-0"

33'-0"

36'-5"

32'-0" OVER BODY

BRAKE HANDLE

BRAKE CYLINDER

A

A

B

B

to the main longitudinals of the underframe, and the upper ends of these clips held the lower flanges of outwardly-facing channel members forming part of the body floor.

Much of the underframe, as well as the axleboxes, made use of welded plate, resulting in a weight saving of 12½ cwt. compared with the frame of a standard luggage van. The weight of each axlebox was reduced from 147½ lb. to 98 lb.

The body frame was made of light 12-gauge steel sections electric-welded in a jig. The plastic panels, reinforced by woven high-tensile steel wire and cotton, weighted only 11½ ounces per square foot. The plastic was black, and the vans ran in this colour for several years before any were painted green. The louvred doors, two pairs per side, were made of No. 16 Standard Wire Gauge sheet steel less than one inch thick.

No further examples of the plastic luggage vans were built, construction reverting to traditional methods. As they were worked indiscriminately with 13-ton vans, any weight saving can hardly have been noticed; it needed far more than 10 vans to make any appreciable difference. Although non-standard all but one lasted until the 1960s.

Some livery details were recorded over the years.

1401: remained black until its withdrawal in August 1958
1402: painted black 1.48 and 5.53 and, probably, green 5.58.
1403: painted black 9.48 and 1.55 (after entering shops 10.53!)
1404: black, later green
1405: black
1406: black
1407: livery recorded as green, not dated
1408: painted black 5.48 and 5.55
1409: livery recorded as green, n.d., painted 7.48, 7.54, 7.57
1410: painted black 5.55

No. 1401 was the first example to be withdrawn, becoming stores van No. 082186 at Eastleigh Carriage Works. Nos. 1405/6 were laid aside in about October 1961, although not formally condemned until December 1963. The last survivor by several years was No. 1402, withdrawn in September 1972.

SUMMARY OF PLASTIC-BODIED LUGGAGE VANS

Built		Withdrawn	Built		Withdrawn
1401	12.43	8.58	1406	6.44	12.63
2	4.44	9.72	7	8.44	12.66
3	5.44	10.67	8	8.44 Mishap, 5.5.60	8.61
4	5.44	2.66	9	8.44	2.66
5	5.44	12.63	1410	9.44	5.63

Notes

1401 renumbered 082186, internal user series, 1964
1405 renumbered 082145, internal user series, 1964.

Plastic-bodied PMV No. 1407, built in August 1944, here shown with BR lettering and in green livery. Newport (WR), 26th October, 1963. *P.H. Swift*

General utility van No. 2028, built by the Midland Railway-Carriage & Wagon Co. in March 1928. Note internal bars protecting the glazing, lozenge-shaped chalking panels and angled ventilator hoods. *Midland R.C. & W.Co.*

Utility van (Van 'U') No. 2051, from the batch of 50 built by the Midland Railway-Carriage & Wagon Co. in 1928. The doors in the end are clearly shown, along with the letter 'A' to indicate that Ashford Works was responsible for repairs. The paint date '3.3.28' is on the solebar at the right-hand end. *Midland R.C. & W.Co.*

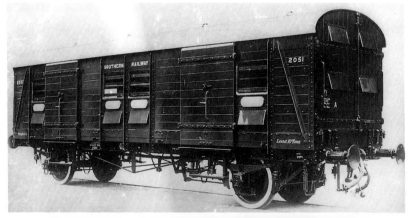

Chapter Six

4-Wheeled Utility Vans

At a meeting of the Rolling Stock Committee on 6th April, 1925, Maunsell proposed a design of general utility van, each vehicle to cost about £800. As the name suggests, such a van could be used to carry almost anything and thus combine the features of passenger luggage vans and covered carriage trucks. They could convey milk in churns, fruit, motor road vehicles, light field guns or aeroplanes; and all the vans hitherto used for these traffics – fruit vans, milk vans, carriage trucks and aeroplane trucks – could be gradually eliminated and money saved.

The design was similar to that of the last South Eastern & Chatham 21 ft-wheelbase type of luggage van, with two sets of double doors each side and four fixed windows (but with the addition of bodyside ventilators, which the SEC vans did not have). For end loading there were outward-opening double doors and a small drop door in each van-end so that road vehicles could be driven straight in. Wheelbars on the floor restrained any further movement once the van was in motion. The body was timber-planked with outside steel strapping and was 32 ft 4¼ in. long; the roof also was of wooden planks, covered with canvas. Overall length and width were 35 ft 10 in. and 8 ft 10⅞ in. and from rail to roof measured 12 ft (Diagram 3101).

Twenty vans were authorised on 29th April, 1925, plus a further 30 on 28th April, 1926. All were built by the Midland Railway Carriage & Wagon Co. at a cost of £659 each and, numbered 2023–72 in the 'luggage van' block instead of the 'covered carriage truck' one, were sent into traffic between March and May 1928, all having been supplied by 25th April. Tare weight was 14 tons. Somewhat confusingly, while they were always referred to as utility vans (coded by the Southern 'Van U') they had the word 'COVCAR' painted on them. British Railways re-styled them 'Covered Carriage Trucks' (CCT).

The design was clearly a success, and so Ashford Works was kept busily employed over the next few years turning out 140 new utility vans. Order No. 277 in March 1927 was for 30 vans, Nos. 2251–80, which were completed between April and July 1929. Several of them had shelves for carrying boxes of fruit. An order was made in April 1929 for 40 vans, Nos. 2371–2410, and these emerged between April and July 1931. They had slightly longer bodies, being 32 ft 6¾ in. instead of 32 ft 4¼ in. in length. Fifty vans (Order No. 574) were ordered in April 1930 and completed by Ashford between September 1931 and February 1932 – Nos. 2411–60. Then, after the next 20 had been authorised in March 1931 (Nos. 2241–50 and 2491–2500) and built between February and April 1933, no more were constructed for another five years.

In March 1937 a batch of 50 utility vans was authorised (Order No. A972), construction work being divided between Ashford for underframes and Eastleigh for bodies. They were built in November and December 1938. There was a change in body styling: instead of equal-width planking there was a curious arrangement of alternate pairs of 3½ in.-wide and 6½ in.-wide planks along the bodyside. Even more oddly, the double doors were, in contrast, equally planked with 6½ in.-wide planks. These utility vans, Nos. 1731–80, were the last to be built by the Southern Railway.

In 1951 the design was revived by BR. Although overall dimensions were identical to those of the Southern Railway vans the main difference was that the BR-built vehicles had plywood bodysides, which made them look extremely unattractive. The doors, however, had to be of stouter construction than the bodysides and so were formed of planking arranged in alternate pairs of 3½ in. and 6½ in. planks. Order No. A3702 was for 100 covered carriage trucks, which were built at Ashford in 1951. Numbering was rather haphazard as gaps left by withdrawn vehicles were filled: Nos. 1411–50, 1977–91, 2006–20, 2073–82, 2171–80 and 2231–40.

The final order for covered carriage trucks came as late as 1955, and these were the very last vans of SR design to be built. Order No. L3764 was dealt with by Lancing Works: a batch of 50 CCTs, Nos. 2501–50, with plywood bodysides as on the 1951 batch, the last being completed in November 1955. They had wood-planked floors.

Utility Van Working

From September 1929 the 1.30 am Waterloo to Plymouth news train included a Van U, which was detached at Salisbury and forwarded to Templecombe at 3.15 am. The 6.30 am Exeter to Waterloo also included a Van U, as did the 10.30 pm Waterloo to Dorchester as far as Bournemouth Central. On Sundays the 3.30 am from Waterloo included a van for Havant.

From July 1930 a Van U worked in the 7.30 am Bournemouth West to Waterloo with a LSW bogie van and a 6-coach corridor dining set. The 10.30 pm conveyed a van for Southampton Terminus.

By September 1931 the 11.35 am empty churn train from Clapham Junction included a Van U for Salisbury, thence Sturminster Newton via Templecombe. The 3.15 am empty churn train from Waterloo had a van for Semley and two for Seaton Junction. The 7.45 am Waterloo to Petersfield had one, as did the 10.30 am Exeter to Waterloo (leading vehicle).

The May 1936 carriage workings show that the 1.30 am still had its Van U for Salisbury thence Templecombe; the 3.00 am from Waterloo had two for Portsmouth & Southsea and one for Poole; the 3.08 am had one for Andover Junction, conveying parcels; and the 3.45 am had one for Bournemouth Central, except Mondays, and one for Guildford. Many Western Section passenger trains conveyed at least one utility van, as study of photographs will show.

On the Central Section in 1930 it is recorded that van No. 2266 was specially allocated for poultry traffic between Heathfield and London Bridge. During the day it was loaded at Heathfield, leaving there at 8.21 pm for Eastbourne. From Eastbourne it left at 9.50 pm for London Bridge via Brighton and Redhill. Next morning the empty crates were loaded at London Bridge and the van left on the rear of the 8.03 am Oxted line train, being detached at Oxted and attached to the 9.06 am to Tunbridge Wells West. It finally arrived at Heathfield on the 10.40 am from Tunbridge Wells West and the cycle continued.

In general, however, utility vans tended to be employed indiscriminately with passenger luggage vans, especially in later years, and it was rare for them to be allocated special diagrams.

Some records of wartime damage have survived. On 14th August, 1940 No. 2376 was damaged by enemy action while on the 3.05 pm Bournemouth to Waterloo, and the high-explosive bomb that fell on Clapham Junction carriage sheds on 8th September, 1940 damaged No. 2034, among other vehicles. On 7th November, 1940 Nos. 1780 and 2243 were damaged at Bricklayers Arms. All were subsequently repaired.

BR Livery Changes

Vans continued to be painted green until 1949, when British Railways red was stipulated for all further repaints until 1956, although some vans managed to escape being painted red. Some examples are shown below:

2252 painted red 3.52, green 5.58
2254 painted red 1952, was never green after then
2257 painted red 3.53, green 6.56
2372 painted red 1.56 (one of the last), did not return to green
2376 was never painted red

Withdrawals

Withdrawals began in earnest in 1962, when almost the whole of the 2023–72 and 2251–80 series were condemned (a few lasted until 1963). Many were converted to departmental vehicles. Nos. 2241–50, 2371–2460 and 2491–2500 lasted until the mid- and late-1960s, and a few were retained for departmental use, mainly stores vans. Most of the 1938 series were withdrawn in the early 1980s, and the last two plywood-bodied vans were withdrawn in February 1986 (Nos. 2239 and 2516).

Ten CCTs are known to have been purchased by private railways for preservation or other uses:

1418 body only to Brecon Mountain Railway, Pontsticill, 1976
1745 to Kent & East Sussex Railway, 3.82; locomotive department van
1750 to Isle of Wight Steam Railway, 11.81; required for underframe only
1768 to Mid-Hants Railway, 7.77
2239 to North Downs Steam Railway, Stone Lodge, 5.87
2276 to Bluebell Railway (as DS70202), 8.74; S&T workshop
2439 to Cholsey & Wallingford Railway (as DS70324), 1989
2504 body only to Brecon Mountain Railway, Pontsticill, 1976
2524 body only to Brecon Mountain Railway, Pontsticill, 1976
2531 to Bluebell Railway, 8.81; Camelot Society workshop

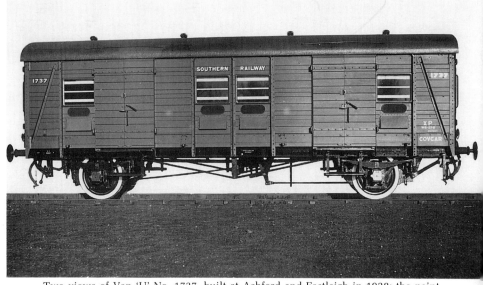

Two views of Van 'U' No. 1737, built at Ashford and Eastleigh in 1938; the paint-date '22.11.38' is visible on the solebar. Note that although the bodyside is planked with alternate pairs of wide and narrow planks the doors have planks of equal width.

M.S. King

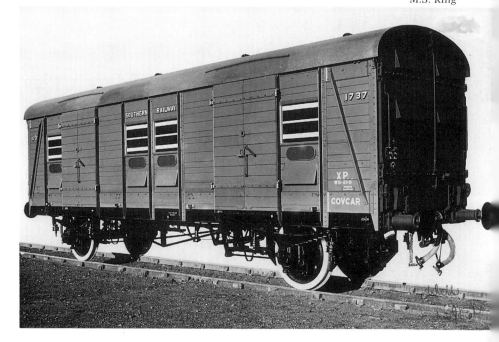

Van 'U' (BR CCT) in working condition at East Croydon post office siding on 9th September, 1977. No. 1753 was built at Ashford (*underframe*) and Eastleigh (*body*) in November 1938. The two vans shown had arrived on the 4.55 am from Bricklayers Arms, and would continue to Redhill at 9.52 pm.
Author

Details of left-hand corner of CCT No. 2427 (built at Ashford in January 1932), which became departmental vehicle No. DS 70292 in March 1970. The Porchester Road address shown was better known as the location of British Transport Historical Records.
Author

Plywood-bodied CCT No. 2527, built at Lancing in October 1955, here shown as 'Hither Green Packing Van' No. ADB 977010, to which it was renumbered in February 1982. Doors have planks of widths 6½ in. and 3½ in. Stewarts Lane, 10th April, 1988.
Author

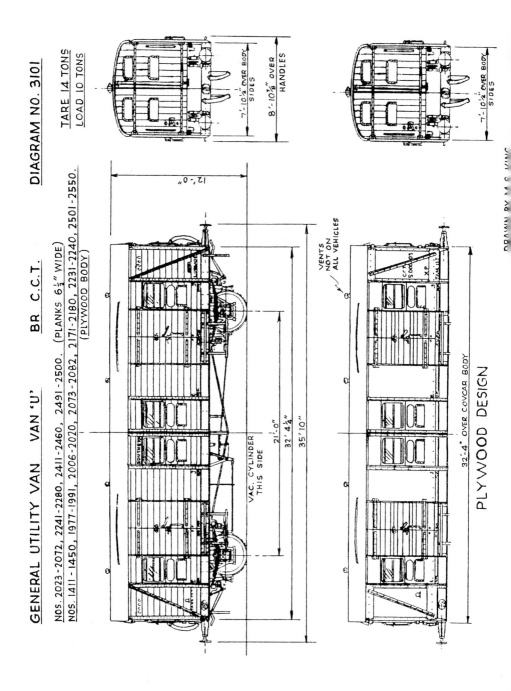

GENERAL UTILITY VAN   VAN 'U'   BR C.C.T.   DIAGRAM NO. 3101

NOS. 2023-2072, 2241-2280, 2411-2460, 2491-2500. (PLANKS 6½" WIDE)
NOS. 1411-1450, 1977-1991, 2006-2020, 2073-2082, 2171-2180, 2231-2240, 2501-2550.
(PLYWOOD BODY)

TARE 14 TONS
LOAD 10 TONS

7'-10½" OVER BODY SIDES

8'-10⅞" OVER HANDLES

12'-0"

VAC. CYLINDER THIS SIDE

21'-0"

32'-4¼"

35'-10"

7'-10½" OVER BODY SIDES

VENTS NOT ON ALL VEHICLES

32'-4" OVER COVCAR BODY

PLYWOOD DESIGN

DRAWN BY M.S. KING

4-WHEELED UTILITY VANS
Summary of Building and Withdrawal Dates

Built	Withdrawn	Built	Withdrawn
1731 11.38	7.68	1776 12.38 Bricklayers Arms	5.81
2 11.38	c.8.81	7 11.38	by 3.81
3 11.38	8.82	8 12.38	c.8.81
4 11.38	c.4.81	9 11.38 Margam	3.81
5 11.38 Margam	3.81	1780 11.38	11.82
6 11.38	11.71	1411 12.51	c.5.81
7 11.38 Margam	3.81	2 12.51 Fire damage	11.73
8 11.38	c.9.81	3 12.51	4.82
9 11.38	c.5.81	4 12.51 To 041683,	
1740 12.38	10.82	3.84	
1 11.38	c.8.81	5 10.51	c.10.81
2 11.38	11.72	6 10.51	c.3.81
3 11.38	3.72	7 12.51	c.8.81
4 11.38	10.82	8 12.51	c.12.80
5 11.38	6.81	9 12.51	10.82
6 12.38	c.2.81	1420 11.51	c.8.81
7 11.38 To DB975276,	84	1 11.51	c.5.81
73		2 11.51	c.5.81
8 11.38	6.82	3 10.51	c.11.81
9 11.38	2.82	4 12.51	10.82
1750 11.38	c.8.81	5 11.51	c.8.81
1 11.38 Margam	3.81	6 11.51	c.8.81
2 11.38	81	7 10.51	82
3 11.38 Bricklayers Arms	5.81	8 10.51	c.7.81
4 11.38	6.76	9 10.51	c.7.81
5 11.38	by 3.81	1430 12.51	10.82
6 11.38	10.72	1 12.51 Margam	3.81
7 12.38	9.68	2 12.51	c.8.81
8 11.38	by 3.81	3 10.51	9.82
9 12.38	c.4.81	4 10.51 Cardiff	1.81
1760 12.38	c.10.81	5 10.51	4.83
1 12.38	2.82	6 12.51	by 3.81
2 12.38	c.3.81	7 12.51	c.8.81
3 12.38	c.5.81	8 12.51 Bricklayers Arms	5.81
4 12.38	c.7.81	9 11.51	1.86
5 12.38	c.8.81	1440 11.51	c.5.81
6 12.38	7.80	1 11.51	c.5.81
7 12.38	c.7.81	2 12.51 Margam	3.81
8 11.38 Eastleigh	4.77	3 12.51 Margam	3.81
9 11.38 Bricklayers Arms	5.81	4 12.51	5.82
1770 11.38 To 024534,		5 12.51	5.82
5.86		6 12.51	c.3.81
1 11.38 Stonebridge Park	5.81	7 11.51 Margam	3.81
2 11.38	3.66	8 12.51	5.82
3 11.38	c.5.81	9 12.51	9.82
4 11.38	10.82	1450 12.51	c.5.81
5 11.38	c.10.81	1977 12.51	2.82

Built	Withdrawn	Built	Withdrawn
1978 12.51	10.82	2034 4.28	12.62
9 12.51	80	5 3.28 To DS70222,	c.84
1980 11.51	12.82	c.64	
1 11.51	c.7.81	6 5.28	12.62
2 11.51	2.82	7 4.28	12.62
3 12.51	c.11.81	8 3.28	12.62
4 11.51	5.82	9 4.28 Underframe to	
5 11.51	c.8.81	082031, 1.64	
6 11.51 Margam	3.81	2040 4.28 To DS70207,	89
7 11.51 To 083431,	c.89	12.63	
c.82		1 4.28 Underframe to	12.62
8 11.51	79	082033, 1.64	
9 11.51 To ADB977039,	84	2 4.28 To DS70197,	3.72
10.81		4.63	
1990 12.51	by 3.81	3 4.28	12.62
1 11.51	10.82	4 4.28	12.62
2006 11.51	by 3.81	5 4.28	12.62
7 12.51	c.11.81	6 4.28 To DS70214,	c.84
8 11.51	c.5.81	6.64	
9 12.51	c.10.81	7 4.28 To DS70219,	c.84
2010 10.51	2.86	64	
1 10.51	6.82	8 4.28 Underframe to	
2 10.51	c.11.81	082029, 12.63	
3 11.51	10.82	9 4.28	12.62
4 11.51	1.82	2050 4.28 To 082229,	
5 10.51	c.6.81	11.64	
6 10.51	c.5.81	1 4.28 To DS70220,	
7 11.51	82	c.64	
8 11.51 Sold to	78	2 4.28	12.62
Central Wagon		3 4.28	12.62
Co., Ince		4 4.28	12.62
9 10.51	by 3.81	5 4.28	12.62
2020 12.51 Burnt out Roade,	7.73	6 4.28	12.62
3.10.72		7 4.28	12.62
2023 5.28	12.62	8 4.28	12.62
4 3.28	12.62	9 4.28	12.62
5 3.28 Underframe to		2060 4.28	12.62
082030, 1.64		1 4.28	12.62
6 3.28 To 081814,		2 4.28	12.62
11.64		3 4.28	7.64
7 3.28	12.62	4 4.28 To Barrier Wagon	?
8 3.28	12.62	69000, 7.65	
9 3.28	12.62	5 4.28	12.62
2030 3.28 Underframe to		6 4.28	12.62
082032, 1.64		7 4.28	12.62
1 4.28	12.62	8 4.28 To Barrier Wagon	?
2 4.28	12.62	69003, 7.65	
3 4.28	12.62	9 4.28	12.62

Built	Withdrawn	Built	Withdrawn
2070 4.28	12.62	2254 6.29 To 082047,	
1 4.28	12.62	1.64	
2 4.28	12.62	5 5.29	12.62
3 12.51	c.8.81	6 4.29	12.62
4 11.51 Severn Tunnel Jn	4.82	7 6.29 To 081646,	
5 11.51	c.10.81	c.63	
6 11.51	c.8.81	8 4.29	12.62
7 11.51	c.10.81	9 7.29	12.62
8 12.51	6.82	2260 4.29 To Barrier Wagon	
9 11.51	c.9.81	69002, c.65	
2080 11.51	c.5.81	1 7.29	12.62
1 10.51	6.82	2 6.29 To 081640,	
2 10.51 Bricklayers Arms	5.81	3.63	
2171 12.51	2.82	3 6.29 To Barrier Wagon	
2 12.51	c.8.81	69006, c.65	
3 12.51	4.82	4 6.29 To Barrier Wagon	
4 12.51	3.82	69009, 8.65	
5 11.51 Bricklayers Arms	5.81	5 6.29 To Barrier Wagon	
6 11.51 Bricklayers Arms	5.81	69005, c.65	
7 11.51	c.10.81	6 6.29	12.62
8 10.51 Bricklayers Arms	5.81	7 7.29	12.62
9 10.51	c.10.81	8 7.29 To Barrier Wagon	12.62
2180 10.51	10.82	69008, c. 65	
2231 12.51	c.5.81	9 4.29	12.62
2 12.51	by 3.81	2270 4.29 To DS70221,	6.77
3 11.51	c.6.81	2.65	
4 11.51	4.72	accident damage	
5 11.51	by 3.81	Rowlands Castle	
6 11.51	81	10.8.76; broken	
7 10.51	c.78	up on site	
8 11.51	81	1 6.29	12.62
9 10.51	2.86	2 6.29	12.62
2240 11.51	c.11.81	3 6.29 To 81645,	
1 4.33	11.65	1.63	
2 4.33 To DS70263,		4 5.29	12.62
c.67		5 5.29	12.62
3 4.33	1.67	6 5.29 To DS70202,	9.73
4 4.33	5.68	4.63	
5 4.33	9.64	7 7.29 To DS70203,	5.76
6 4.33	1.67	4.63	
7 2.33	1.67	8 7.29 To Barrier Wagon	
8 2.33	7.69	69001, c.65	
9 2.33	11.67	9 4.29 To Barrier Wagon	
2250 2.33	1.67	69004, c.65	
1 5.29	12.62	2280 7.29	12.62
2 6.29	12.62	2371 6.31	8.68
3 6.29	12.62	2 6.31 To DS70240,	9.68
		3.66	

Built		Withdrawn	Built		Withdrawn
2373	6.31 To DS70239, 66		2410	4.31 To DS70241, 3.66	11.71
4	6.31 Underframe to DS70252, 4.67		1	11.31 To DS70249, c.66	
5	6.31	5.66	2	11.31	1.67
6	5.31	6.68	3	1.32 To DS70231, 10.65	3.72
7	6.31	6.56	4	1.32	5.67
8	5.31	1.67	5	11.31	6.68
9	6.31 To DS70274, 9.68 accident damage Crewe, 8.69 broken up, 10.69		6	1.32	1.67
			7	1.32	5.64
			8	1.32	4.67
			9	1.32	11.65
2380	5.31	1.67	2420	1.32	6.67
1	6.31	1.67	1	1.32	6.68
2	6.31	1.66	2	1.32	4.67
3	5.31	8.65	3	1.32 To DS70243, 66	c.89
4	5.31	12.68	4	12,31	1.67
5	7.31	11.65	5	12.31	1.67
6	7.31	2.66	6	12.31	1.67
7	6.31	1.67	7	1.32 To DS70292, 3.70	12.78
8	6.31	1.67	8	12.31	1.67
9	6.31	5.67	9	12.31	12.66
2390	6.31	3.70	2430	9.31	1.67
1	6.31	1.67	1	1.32 To DS70242, c.66	
2	6.31	5.66	2	10.31	1.67
3	6.31	1.67	3	10.31 To DS70250, 8.66	11.71
4	6.31	1.66	4	10.31 Underframe to DS70253, 4.67	
5	6.31	1.67	5	1.32	1.67
6	6.31	1.67	6	1.32	1.67
7	4.31	1.67	7	2.32	5.67
8	4.31	7.67	8	9.31	1.67
9	4.31	1.67	9	9.31 To DS70324, c.70	89
2400	6.31 To 082949, 1.71		2440	11.31 Underframe to DS70254, 2.67	c.89
1	6.31 To 082205, c.66		1	9.31	6.68
2	5.31	1.67	2	10.31	4.67
3	5.31 To 082287, c.67		3	10.31	1.67
4	5.31	1.67	4	12.31	1.67
5	5.31	1.65	5	10.31 To 081339, c.66	
6	5.31	12.65			
7	5.31	12.66			
8	4.31	1.67			
9	5.31	7.65			

Built	Withdrawn	Built	Withdrawn
2446 10.31 To 082979, c.71		2511 7.55	10.82
		2 7.55	c.11.81
7 10.31	6.64	3 7.55	c.8.81
8 10.31	1.66	4 7.55	c.7.81
9 9.31 Underframe to DS70255, 5.67		5 8.55	c.10.81
		6 9.55	2.86
2450 11.31	10.65	7 8.55	c.7.81
1 12.31	2.67	8 9.55	7.85
2 12.31	2.67	9 9.55	c.5.81
3 12.31	2.67	2520 9.55	c.8.81
4 12.31	12.68	1 9.55	by 3.81
5 10.31	2.67	2 9.55	c.8.81
6 9.31	12.66	3 9.55 Damaged Horsham	5.58
7 9.31	2.67	4 9.55	6.82
8 9.31 To DS70282, 5.69	3.70	5 9.55	c.10.81
		6 9.55	6.82
9 9.31	12.65	7 10.55 To ADB977010, 2.82	c.89
2460 9.31	2.67		
2491 2.33 Damaged Royton, 28.8.61	12.61	8 10.55	c.8.81
		9 10.55	c.6.81
2 2.33	3.70	2530 10.55	c.11.81
3 3.33	2.69	1 10.55 Bricklayers Arms	5.81
4 3.33	5.66	2 10.55 Severn Tunnel Jn	4.82
5 3.33 To DS70265, 8.68 Damaged Ton-bridge, 11.80	1.81	3 10.55	c.10.81
		4 10.55	c.11.81
		5 10.55	c.5.81
6 3.33	11.65	6 10.55	c.3.81
7 3.33 To DS70264, c.68	c.89	7 11.55	c.12.80
		8 11.55	2.68
8 3.33	2.67	9 11.55 Margam	3.81
9 4.33	4.67	2540 12.55	c.11.81
2500 4.33	8.69	1 11.55 Damaged Royton, 3.7.63	8.63
1 6.55	80		
2 6.55	10.82	2 12.55	c.10.81
3 7.55	by 3.81	3 11.55	2.83
4 7.55	c.3.81	4 11.55	c.3.81
5 7.55	3.82	5 11.55	81
6 7.55 Margam	3.81	6 11.55	c.8.81
7 7.55	81	7 12.55 Severn Tunnel Jn	4.82
8 7.55	by 3.81	8 12.55	c.11.81
9 7.55 To 083432, 82	c.89	9 12.55 Whittlesea	3.81
		2550 12.55	9.81
2510 7.55	c.5.81		

Notes

Another source states 2491 mishap Dallam 28.8.61 and 2541 damaged Desborough 3.7.63.

Bogie luggage van No. 2319, built at Ashford in September 1930 on the underframe of an ex-LSW coach of 1906. Note handbrake wheel, dynamo for electric lighting, wooden-segmented wheels, the letter 'A' for Ashford on the end, and the British Standard gangways with adaptors enabling them to work with Pullman-gangwayed coaching stock. *Courtesy National Railway Museum*

Bogie luggage van No. 2326, built at Ashford in October 1930 on the underframe of an ex-LSW coach of 1904. This view is of the opposite side to that of No. 2319, so that the dynamo is now seen at the left-hand end and the handbrake wheel at the right-hand end. *Courtesy National Railway Museum*

Chapter Seven
Bogie Luggage Vans

During 1927 and 1928 many of the ex-London & South Western 'bogie block' suburban 4-coach sets were converted into 3-coach DC electric units and 2-coach trailer sets, using the old bodies mounted on new 62 ft underframes. The LSW underframes were not discarded, because it was realised that they would be good enough to use for a series of gangwayed bogie luggage vans that was proposed.

The first 50 of these were authorised in April 1928. The bodies, of timber planking with outside steel frames, were effectively a stretched version of the 4-wheeled SR luggage vans, with three sets of double doors and six fixed windows each side. British Standard scissor-type gangways were fitted, with adaptors to enable them to be coupled to Pullman-gangwayed coaching stock. The bodies, each 51 ft 3 in. long and 7 ft 10¾ in. wide, were built at Ashford between March and October 1930 (Order No. 443, Diagram No. 3100) and mounted on 51 ft underframes taken from 7-compartment third brakes and 8-compartment composites built between 1902 and 1912. Ashford had converted the bodies of these coaches into DC electric units during 1928, but some had been done at Lancing and Eastleigh, whence the old underframes would have had to be worked specially to Ashford. The new vans received the numbers 2281–2330; tare weight was 26 tons.

The next batch of vans was authorised in April 1929 and built at Ashford between November 1930 and May 1931. This order covered two slightly different types. Nos. 2331–54 (Diagram 3098) used 51 ft 3 in. bodies mounted on the underframes of 49 ft 'block' 8-compartment composites lengthened by about 2 ft; and Nos. 2355–70 (Diagram 3099) used 53 ft 3 in. bodies on the underframes of more 51 ft third brakes and composites, but lengthened by about 2 ft. Bogie centres were 34 ft 3 in. for Diagram 3098 and 36 ft 3 in. for Diagrams 3099 and 3100. Again, tare weight was 26 tons.

A final batch of 30 corridor vans was authorised in April 1930 for completion in 1931 (Order No. 573). Once again, lengthened 49 ft and 51 ft underframes from 'block' sets were used: Nos. 2461–81 had 53 ft 3 in. bodies (Diagram 3099) and Nos. 2482–90, using the frames from 49 ft composites, had 51 ft 3 in. bodies (Diagram 3098). Ashford constructed all these bodies between July and September 1931.

The original bogies were retained; coil springs replaced the elliptical bolster springs, but the original Mansell wheels, with their wooden segments, were retained. The vans – coded 'GBL' by the Southern – were painted green with white roof and black ends and underframe. Lettering was mid-chrome yellow on the body, but any lettering on the solebar was done in white.

GBL Vans were used largely on the Western Section, although there were a few on the Eastern Section too, working in parcels trains or occasionally in passenger trains on the Chatham main line. Two vans, when still new, were seen in the 10.44 am train from Ashford to Victoria via Maidstone East and Swanley Junction on 14th January, 1931. Probably they had only just been sent into traffic from Ashford Works.

From 1931 the 1.30 am newspaper train from Waterloo to the West of England included several new GBL vans: one for Devonport, one for Bude, one for Exeter, one for Ilfracombe and two for Salisbury, of which one was worked forward to Exeter by a later train. The 3.0 am van train from Waterloo had a GBL for Southampton Terminus, one for Portsmouth & Southsea via Eastleigh, one for Southampton West and one for Bournemouth West. A van for Basingstoke ran in the 3.15 am from Waterloo, and the 5.27 am passenger train Waterloo to Portsmouth had a GBL for Portsmouth Harbour (except Mondays), one for Portsmouth & Southsea (except Mondays), one for Basingstoke detached at Woking, and one for Southampton via Ropley, not Mondays. The 11.30 am and 7.30 pm Bournemouth trains each had a GBL for Southampton Terminus included. Coming up, single vans were included in the 8.21 am from Portsmouth & Southsea, 8.35 am from Bournemouth West, 6.30 and 10.30 am from Exeter, and 6.30 pm from Weymouth. On Sundays, the 3.30 am from Waterloo included a GBL for Portsmouth & Southsea, one for Havant, thence Brighton, and one for Southampton West. All these were in direct replacement of ex-LSW bogie vans.

By May 1936 the 3.0 am from Waterloo included a van for Southampton Terminus except Mondays, one for Portsmouth Harbour, one for Portsmouth & Southsea, one for Bournemouth West, one for Weymouth and one for Southampton Central (formerly Southampton West). Many more trains working into and out of Waterloo were booked to include GBL vans, the number in any given train often varying per day of the week.

Many were the uses to which GBL vans were put, carrying newspapers, parcels, milk churns or even bicycles. In 1938 the *Southern Railway Magazine* reported that a cyclists' special train had worked from Waterloo to Winchester formed of six coaches and four corridor luggage vans. The vans accommodated a total of 160 bicycles and no special racks had been fitted.

During 1938 and 1939 vans Nos. 2341/2 were reserved for conveying dairy products from the Yeovil depot of Aplin & Barrett. The vans carried roof-boards and were stencilled on the solebars: 'To work between Yeovil and London'. Each van worked, on alternate days, the following diagram:

> 1.30 am Waterloo to Salisbury, thence 3.15 am to Yeovil. 6.40 pm (SX), 7.40 pm (SO) Yeovil to Yeovil Junction, thence 7.08 pm (SX), 8.1 pm (SO) to Waterloo (attached to 5.55 pm from Exeter).

The contract was cancelled in August 1939.

In 1939 five more GBL vans were specially reserved for regular working, this time for Wilts United Dairies' traffic in milk churns. These vans, stencilled 'To be returned to Chard Junction', were Nos. 2300, 2315, 2322, 2326 and 2470. There were three diagrams, the first two of which required two vans each, working on a 2-day cycle, and the third requiring one van working on a 3-day cycle shared with two London & North Eastern vans.

> 1.   11.37 am Chard Jn to Taunton, thence 12.56 pm to Crewe. 3.50 am (MX) Crewe to Bristol, 12.35 pm Bristol to Taunton, thence 6.48 pm to Chard Jn. On Sundays worked 11.5 am Crewe to Bristol, for 12.35 pm etc. on Mondays.

2.   4.55 pm (SX) Chard Junction to Taunton, thence 6.12 pm to Crewe. 3.50 am (MX) Crewe to Bristol, 12.35 pm (MX) Bristol to Taunton, thence 6.48 pm to Chard Jn.

3.   12.52 pm Chard Jn to Taunton, 4.9 pm Taunton to Westbury, 5.20 pm Westbury to Glasgow.
Next day from Glasgow to York, thence 10.13 pm to Bristol.
Next day 12.35 pm Bristol to Taunton, thence 6.48 pm (SX), 5.25 pm (SO) to Chard Jn.

Later in 1939, at the request of the Ministry of Health, the SR made up three Casualty Evacuation Trains. Each train comprised two ex-SEC corridor brake composites and 10 stretcher vans modified from the corridor luggage vans. By October 1939 one of the stretcher vans in each train had been replaced by an SR-built 'nondescript' saloon, but the intention was to replace these as soon as possible by ex-LSW restaurant cars. Each stretcher van contained two fire extinguishers and a bell push near the middle of the van operated a bell simultaneously in each composite brake coach. These modifications were carried out at Lancing Works.

In total there were 34 Casualty Evacuation Trains made up by all the 'Big Four' railways; the Southern's were Nos. 32, 33 and 34. Their formations in October 1939 were:

	No. 32	No. 33	No. 34
Cor. Bke Cpo	6628	6626	6633
GBL Stretcher	2358	2356	2473
,,	2370	2464	2462
,,	2366	2477	2463
,,	2359	2469	2471
,,	2360	2475	2465
,,	2363	2369	2361
,,	2466	2367	2368
,,	2480	2468	2364
,,	2461	2472	2357
Nondescript	7794	7910	7982
Cor. Bke Cpo	6630	6635	6629

The stretcher vans were returned to traffic as luggage vans in October/November 1945.

Later in the War some GBL vans were converted to ambulance coaches and renumbered; after the War they reverted to their original numbers. Those recorded were:

2335 to 6705 between 1.43 and 7.45
2337 to 6708 between 6.44 and 8.45
2339 to 3609 between 2.44 and 1.47
2369 to 4708 between 9.44 and 4.46
2468 to 4704 between 9.44 and 3.46
2474 to 6809 between 1.45 and 8.45
2486 to 3607 between 2.44 and 2.47

In 1942 No. 2312 was appropriated for ARP use and renumbered 1620S, reverting to its original number in 1945.

Some vans were damaged by enemy action during the War, but all were repaired and returned to traffic. Those recorded include No. 2283, damaged by a high-explosive bomb at Clapham Junction on 8th September, 1940; No. 2327, severely scorched by an incendiary at Rotherhithe Road carriage depot on 12th January, 1941; and No. 2352, very badly damaged by incendiaries at Portsmouth & Southsea on 4th May, 1941. At least one (No. 2353) received replacement body planking in the 'wide-and-narrow alternate pairs' style.

In 1945, droplights were fitted to the centre pair of doors of several vehicles in the 2331–70 and 2461–90 series, those examples of Diagram 3098 that were so modified becoming Diagram 3096, and those of Diagram 3099 becoming 3097. Many of the underframes, which were getting rather tired, needed repairs between 1945 and 1948. Steel disc wheels replaced the old Mansell wheels. When the 'Golden Arrow' Pullman train from Victoria to Dover Marine was reintroduced after the War, one of the modified corridor luggage vans was usually the front vehicle of the down train until 1960.

The British Railways livery changes saw the vans wearing 'crimson lake' and the repaint dates of a few vans have been recorded. No. 2292 was the first to be painted red, in May 1949; 2302 was done in August 1949; 2351 in November 1949; and 2281 in April 1952. Few are recorded as returning to green, the official livery from 1956 onwards; No. 2351 was so-repainted in August 1956; No. 2302 became green (not dated) and No. 2318 was outshopped for the last time in January 1959.

Almost all the vans were withdrawn very rapidly during 1959 and 1960, but a few survived for pigeon traffic. In those days a common sight on many stations was that of a porter releasing racing pigeons from wicker baskets which had arrived by train. The vans stencilled 'For Pigeon Traffic Only' were Nos. 2290, 2331, 2333, 2344, 2347, 2349, 2356, 2358, 2464, 2476, 2487 and 2488. These were withdrawn in November 1961.

No. 2464 achieved fame by being used on 30th January, 1965, to convey the body of Sir Winston Churchill between Waterloo and Handborough (WR), the van being formed in a special 5-car Pullman funeral train. The van had been painted in Pullman car livery expressly for this purpose and bore the paint dates 7.62 and 1.65. Soon afterwards, No. 2464 was purchased by the 'City of Industry', Los Angeles, California, for £350; it was moved from Battersea to Royal Victoria Dock and departed for the USA on 28th October, 1965. It was last heard of in 1978, when it was noted in store at San Pedro, California.

Some of the withdrawn vans were reused in departmental service, their gangways being removed, but all have now been withdrawn. Two were sold for preservation: DS70076 (formerly 2339) to the Kent & East Sussex Railway in May 1982 and DS70141 (formerly 2462) to the Bluebell Railway in August 1981. The Bluebell restored its example to Southern livery in 1982 and reinstated the gangways and fitted electric lighting during the following year.

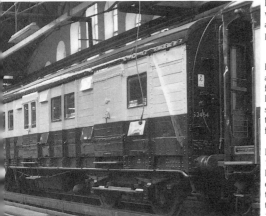

Bogie luggage van No. 2353 (Ashford, April 1931), which has been rebodied at some stage with 6½ in. and 3½ in. planking. It was still in red livery when photographed at Exeter on 29th October, 1959.
A.E. West

Bogie van No. 2464, built at Ashford in July 1931 on an ex-LSW underframe of 1905. Droplights were fitted in the centre pair of doors in 1945. After a brief life as a pigeon van, the vehicle was withdrawn and set aside as a hearse van, painted brown and cream to match Pullman cars and used in Churchill's funeral train on 30th January, 1965.
M.S. King

Bogie van No. 2462 was built at Ashford in August 1931 and transferred to the service vehicles list as DS 70141 in August 1961. It was modified with extra-wide pairs of doors, as shown in this view of the vehicle, which has been restored to SR livery by the Bluebell Railway. Horsted Keynes, 5th August, 1990.
Author

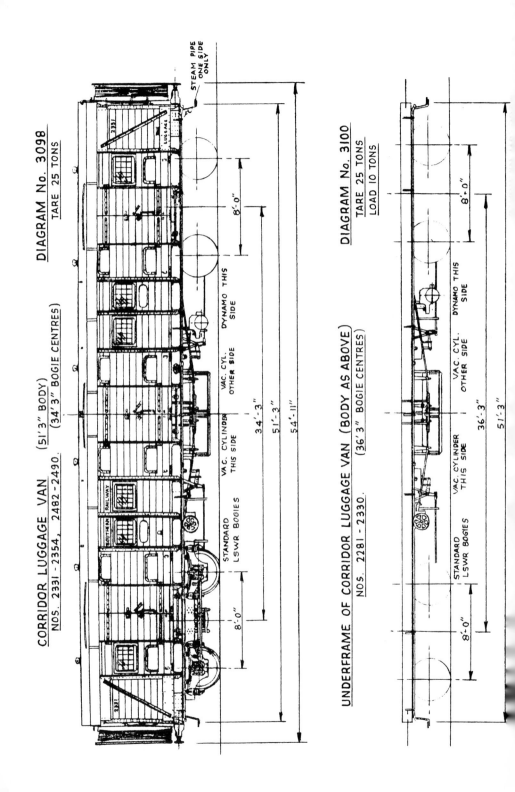

CORRIDOR LUGGAGE VAN   (51' 3" BODY)   DIAGRAM No. 3098
NOS. 2331 - 2354, 2482 - 2490.   (34' 3" BOGIE CENTRES)   TARE 25 TONS

STEAM PIPE
ONE SIDE
ONLY

SOUTHERN RAILWAY

STANDARD
LSWR BOGIES

VAC. CYLINDER
THIS SIDE

VAC. CYL.
OTHER SIDE

DYNAMO THIS
SIDE

8'- 0"
8'- 0"
34'- 3"
51'- 3"
54'- 11"

UNDERFRAME OF CORRIDOR LUGGAGE VAN (BODY AS ABOVE)   DIAGRAM No. 3100
NOS. 2281 - 2330.   (36' 3" BOGIE CENTRES)   TARE 25 TONS
                                                LOAD 10 TONS

STANDARD
LSWR BOGIES

VAC. CYLINDER
THIS SIDE

VAC. CYL.
OTHER SIDE

DYNAMO THIS
SIDE

8'- 0"
8'- 0"
36'- 3"
51'- 3"

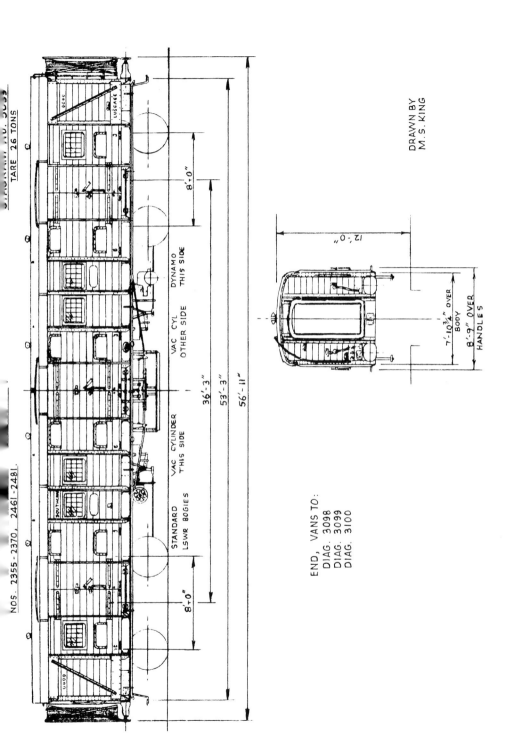

DIAGRAM NO. 3099

TARE 26 TONS

NOS. 2355-2370, 2461-2481.

LUGGAGE

SOUTH

DYNAMO
THIS SIDE

VAC CYL
OTHER SIDE

8'-0"

36'-3"

53'-3"

56'-11"

VAC CYLINDER
THIS SIDE

STANDARD
LSWR BOGIES

8'-0"

END, VANS TO:
DIAG. 3098
DIAG. 3099
DIAG. 3100

12'-0"

7'-10¾" OVER
BODY

8'-9" OVER
HANDLES

DRAWN BY
M. S. KING

BOGIE LUGGAGE VANS
Summary of Building and Withdrawal Dates

Built		Underframe ex	Built	Withdrawn	Remarks
2281	3.30	SR 2885 3rd Bke	12.05	12.59	
2	3.30	LSW 1336 3rd Bke	2.05	10.60	
3	3.30	LSW 2917 Compo	2.05	7.59	
4	3.30	LSW 1330 3rd Bke	12.04	10.60	To 081301, 12.61
5	3.30	LSW 2448 Compo	12.04	7.59	
6	3.30	SR 2834 3rd Bke	9.12	12.59	To DS70036, 12.59; wdn 8.68
7	3.30	LSW 1429 3rd Bke	12.03	12.59	
8	3.30	LSW 1947 3rd Bke	12.04	6.59	
9	3.30	LSW 2419 Compo	2.04	12.58	To 081043, c. 1959
2290	3.30	LSW 1334 3rd Bke	2.05	11.61	To 081616, c. 1962
1	4.30	LSW 1728 3rd Bke	3.04	5.60	
2	4.30	SR 2832 3rd Bke	8.12	12.59	
3	4.30	LSW 1754 3rd Bke	12.04	12.59	
4	4.30	LSW 3002 Compo	5.05	8.59	
5	4.30	LSW 1306 3rd Bke	3.04	8.59	
6	5.30	LSW 2449 Compo	3.04	2.59	
7	5.30	LSW 3004 Compo	6.05		To 300S, 3.46; wdn 9.61
8	5.30	LSW 2277 Compo	12.03	2.59	
9	5.30	LSW 2400 Compo	12.03	3.59	
2300	5.30	LSW 1370 3rd Bke	2.05	2.59	
1	5.30	LSW 1505 3rd Bke	2.04	11.59	
2	6.30	LSW 1948 3rd Bke	12.04	12.59	
3	6.30	LSW 1511 3rd Bke	5.05	11.59	
4	6.30	LSW 1832 3rd Bke	6.05	2.60	
5	6.30	LSW 1822 3rd Bke	5.05	2.62	To 081484, 2.62
6	6.30	LSW 1718 3rd Bke	12.03	11.59	
7	7.30	LSW 2980 Compo	10.03	12.59	
8	6.30	LSW 2981 Compo	11.03	10.60	
9	7.30	LSW 2972 Compo	8.03	3.60	
2310	9.30	LSW 1288 3rd Bke	8.03	12.59	To 081144, c.1960
1	9.30	LSW 1287 3rd Bke	8.03	4.59	
2	8.30	LSW 1833 3rd Bke	6.05		To 1620S, 8.42; to 2312, 12.45; wdn 1.61
3	8.30	SR 4934 Compo	7.03	6.59	
4	8.30	LSW 3000 Compo	5.05	8.59	
5	8.30	SR 2879 3rd Bke	7.03	10.60	
6	8.30	LSW 2472 Compo	12.04	5.59	
7	9.30	LSW 1293 3rd Bke	10.03	8.59	
8	9.30	LSW 1298 3rd Bke	11.03	3.61	
9	9.30	LSW 2560 Compo	5.06	11.59	
2320	9.30	LSW 2998 Compo	4.05	2.59	
1	9.30	LSW 1341 3rd Bke	5.05	9.59	
2	9.30	LSW 2977 Compo	10.03	8.59	
3	10.30	LSW 1344 3rd Bke	6.05	10.59	
4	10.30	SR 2878 3rd Bke	12.05	9.59	
5	10.30	LSW 1639 3rd Bke	12.03	7.59	
6	10.30	LSW 2440 Compo	10.04	9.59	

Built	Underframe ex	Built	Withdrawn	Remarks
7	10.30 SR 2858 3rd Bke	7.03	12.58	To 081044, c.1959
8	10.30 LSW 1321 3rd Bke	3.04	1.60	
9	9.30 LSW 1294 3rd Bke	10.03	11.60	
2330	9.30 LSW 2482 Compo	12.04	7.59	To DS70029, 10.59; wdn 4.63
1	11.30 LSW 2357 Compo	10.04	11.61	
2	11.30 LSW 2484 Compo	3.04	8.60	To DS70083, 8.60; wdn 11.70
3	11.30 LSW 2413 Compo	12.04	11.61	
4	11.30 LSW 2983 Compo	2.04	8.59	
5	11.30 LSW 2997 Compo	4.05	12.59	
6	11.30 LSW 2979 Compo	10.03	8.59	
7	12.30 LSW 2918 Compo	2.05	10.60	
8	12.30 LSW 2992 Compo	2.05	7.59	
9	12.30 LSW 3001 Compo	5.05	12.59	To DS70076, c.60; wdn 81
2340	12.30 SR 4858 Compo	8.12	6.59	
1	11.30 LSW 2978 Compo	10.03	4.59	
2	12.30 LSW 2971 Compo	8.03	9.59	
3	3.31 LSW 2261 Compo	6.05	8.59	
4	3.31 LSW 2916 Compo	2.05	11.61	
5	5.31 LSW 2520 Compo	5.06	10.59	
6	3.31 LSW 2407 Compo	3.04	7.59	
7	12.30 LSW 2995 Compo	5.05	11.61	
8	12.30 LSW 3003 Compo	6.05	6.59	To DS70041, 10.59; wdn 8.65
9	12.30 LSW 2982 Compo	11.03	11.61	
2350	12.30 LSW 2479 Compo	12.03	6.60	
1	1.31 LSW 2999 Compo	5.05	12.59	
2	1.31 LSW 2477 Compo	12.04	9.59	To 081140, c.60
3	4.31 LSW 2293 Compo	6.03	5.60	To 081254, 5.60
4	4.31 LSW 2399 Compo	12.04	6.60	
5	4.31 LSW 2991 Compo	2.05	5.62	
6	4.31 LSW 1902 3rd Bke	12.04	11.61	To 081315, 12.61
7	1.31 LSW 1393 3rd Bke	5.05	3.61	
8	1.31 LSW 2996 Compo	5.05	11.61	
9	1.31 LSW 2919 Compo	2.05	12.59	
2360	4.31 LSW 1954 3rd Bke	2.05	10.59	To 081153, 12.59
1	4.31 LSW 1719 3rd Bke	2.04	2.60	
2	5.31 LSW 1752 3rd Bke	12.04	8.59	
3	5.31 LSW 1342 3rd Bke	5.05	10.59	
4	2.31 LSW 2438 Compo	6.04	12.59	
5	2.31 LSW 1296 3rd Bke	10.03	8.59	
6	3.31 LSW 1859 3rd Bke	3.04	11.59	To 081154, 12.59
7	4.31 LSW 1333 3rd Bke	2.05	6.59	
8	2.31 LSW 1295 3rd Bke	10.03	10.60	
9	2.31 LSW 1343 3rd Bke	5.05	4.60	
2370	1.31 LSW 1297 3rd Bke	11.03	5.61	
2461	8.31 LSW 1410 3rd Bke	12.05	2.60	
2	8.31 LSW 2620 Compo	7.10	10.60	To DS70141, 8.61; wdn 80
3	7.31 LSW 1795 3rd Bke	7.10	7.59	
4	7.31 SR 2869 3rd Bke	10.05	11.61	Reinstated as hearse van

Built	Underframe ex	Built	Withdrawn	Remarks
5	7.31 SR 2833 3rd Bke	8.12	10.60	
6	7.31 SR 4967 Compo	6.05	6.59	
7	7.31 SR 2838 3rd Bke	11.05	7.59	
8	7.31 SR 2803 3rd Bke	11.05	11.60	
9	7.31 LSW 2515 Compo	12.05	10.58	Accident damage Glasgow Buchanan Street, 15.4.58
2470	8.31 SR 2835 3rd Bke	9.12	1.60	
1	7.31 SR 2813 3rd Bke	6.05	7.59	
2	7.31 SR 2825 3rd Bke	10.05	8.59	
3	8.31 SR 4971 Compo	10.05	11.59	
4	7.31 SR 2873 3rd Bke	12.05	5.60	
5	8.31 LSW 1717 3rd Bke	10.05	9.59	
6	8.31 SR 4974 Compo	12.05	11.61	To 081615, 11.62
7	8.31 LSW 1324 3rd Bke	12.05	8.59	
8	8.31 LSW 1335 3rd Bke	2.05	2.59	
9	8.31 SR 2848 3rd Bke	10.05	9.59	
2480	8.31 SR 2861 3rd Bke	12.05	12.59	
1	8.31 SR 4972 Compo	9.12	7.59	
2	8.31 SR 4903 Compo	6.05	9.60	
3	9.31 SR 4866 Compo	12.05	10.59	
4	8.31 SR 4908 Compo	10.05	12.58	Accident damage Exeter, 4.1.58
5	8.31 SR 4869 Compo	9.12	9.59	
6	9.31 LSW 3039 Compo	12.05	1.60	
7	9.31 LSW 3023 Compo	10.05	11.61	
8	9.31 LSW 2619 Compo	7.10	11.61	
9	8.31 SR 4906 Compo	10.05	12.59	
2490	9.31 SR 4911 Compo	12.05	11.59	

Notes

Diagram 3098 altered to Diagram 3096 (droplights in centre doors): Nos. 2333/5/7/9/43/4/6–9/52.

Diagram 3099 altered to Diagram 3097 (droplights in centre doors): Nos. 2355/6/62/5/7/9.

Diagram 3098 altered to Diagram 3096 (droplights in centre doors): Nos. 2482/3/4/6/7/90.

Diagram 3099 altered to Diagram 3097 (droplights in centre doors): Nos. 2464/7/8/9/72/4/5/7/8/9.

Chapter Eight

Special Cattle Vans and Motor Car Van No. 4501

Special cattle vans, used for conveying prize cattle in relative comfort compared with ordinary open-sided cattle trucks, rather resembled horse boxes in appearance. Whereas cattle trucks were classed as goods stock, special cattle vans were definitely passenger-rated stock, being fitted with vacuum and/or Westinghouse air brakes and through steam pipes. The LSW for a time did regard its special cattle vans as goods stock.

The Southern never built any new horse boxes and the very square, short-wheelbase ex-LSW vehicles remained a common sight. However, the need was clearly felt for some new cattle vans as, in April 1929, authority was given to construct 20, each of which, unlike some pre-Grouping designs, included a groom's compartment. In November 1929 a further 30 were authorised and arrangements were made for the whole batch of 50 to be built by the Birmingham Railway Carriage & Wagon Co. (Order No. 529).

The first 30, Nos. 3679–3708, were delivered in June 1930 and the final 20, Nos. 3709–28, arrived the following month. Each one was 4-wheeled, weighed 12 tons, had a body length of 26 ft and wheelbase of 17 ft 6 in. Vacuum and Westinghouse brakes were fitted, as was steam heating. Makeup was two cattle compartments each 10 ft 10 in. long, flanking a central compartment 3 ft 11½ in. long which had a seat for the groom. Illumination was provided by a single oil lamp – a somewhat archaic feature for so late a date as 1930. External livery was passenger green, changed to red in the 1950s; No. 3710 was recorded as receiving BR green in October 1957.

After a long gap of 22 years a further batch of 10 cattle vans was constructed, these being direct replacements of 10 withdrawn pre-Grouping vans. In September and October 1952 Lancing Works built Nos. 3729–38 to Order No. 3706 (Diagram No. 3141); they were identical to the 1930-built vehicles except that they had electric lighting instead of oil. Clearly, no one on what was now the Southern Region of British Railways foresaw in 1952 that in only a few years the conveyance of cattle by rail would cease. Sad to relate, this was the case and withdrawals from the pre-War batch began in 1961; all were gone before the end of 1963. Of these, Nos. 3703/16 were extensively rebuilt as train steam-heating boiler vans in 1962, renumbered DS70191 and DS70190 and allocated to Weymouth. After spending a few years at Oxford (Western Region) they were withdrawn in 1982 and c.1988 respectively.

The BR-built series did not last much longer than the older vans; the first three were withdrawn in 1966 and the last two, Nos. 3733/6, survived until late 1971. After a period of storage at Preston Park, Brighton, No. 3733 was sent on 26th November, 1978, to the Railway Museum at York.

A unique experimental motor car van was constructed at Eastleigh during 1960. It re-used the underframe of Maunsell corridor brake composite No. 6897 and the body, lengthened by the addition of a new section at one end, of corridor luggage van No. 2291. New body ends incorporating double doors for end-loading of motor vehicles had to be fabricated. The van, which was 61 ft 7 in. over buffers, weighed 26 tons and the floor was fitted with

Special cattle van No. 3683, built by Birmingham Railway Carriage & Wagon Co. in June 1930. Dual braked and oil lit; section letter 'E' on the end, to indicate that Eastleigh would be responsible for repairs.   *Courtesy H.R.R.S.*

Special cattle van No. 3700 (Birmingham RC & W Co., June 1930), showing the opposite side to that of No. 3683; note that the window is to the left of the door on this side. Stewarts Lane, 28th May, 1949.   *A.E. West*

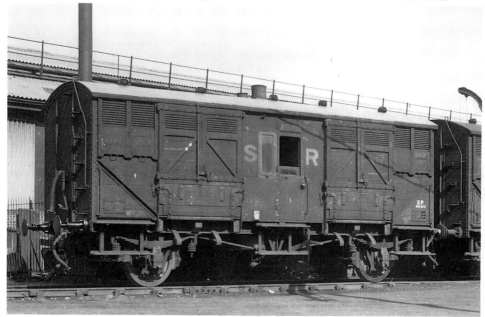

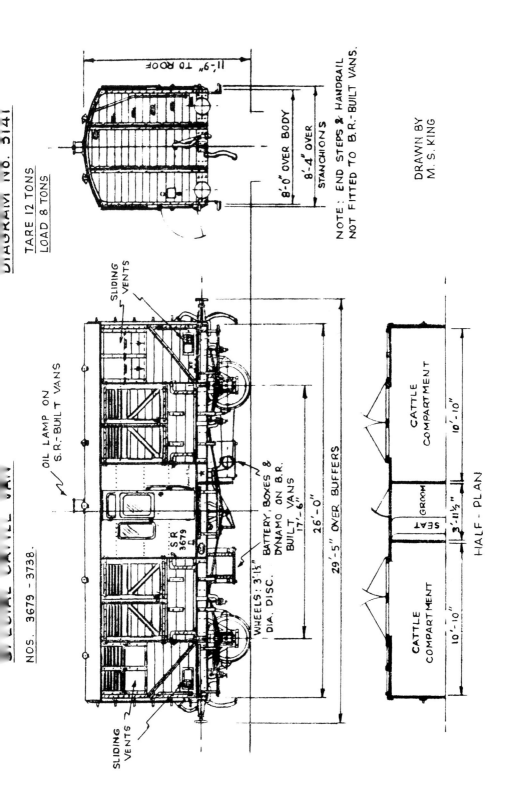

DIAGRAM No. 3141

TARE 12 TONS
LOAD 8 TONS

11'-9" TO ROOF

8'-0" OVER BODY

8'-4" OVER STANCHIONS

NOTE: END STEPS & HANDRAIL
NOT FITTED TO B.R.-BUILT VANS.

DRAWN BY
M. S. KING

SPECIAL CATTLE VAN

NOS. 3679 - 3738.

OIL LAMP ON
S.R.-BUILT VANS

SLIDING VENTS

SLIDING VENTS

SLIDING VENTS

S R
3679

WHEELS: 3'1½"
DIA. DISC.

BATTERY, BOXES &
DYNAMO ON B.R.
BUILT VANS

17'-6"

26'-0"

29'-5" OVER BUFFERS

CATTLE COMPARTMENT

GROOM

SEAT

CATTLE COMPARTMENT

10'-10"

3'-11½"

10'-10"

HALF - PLAN

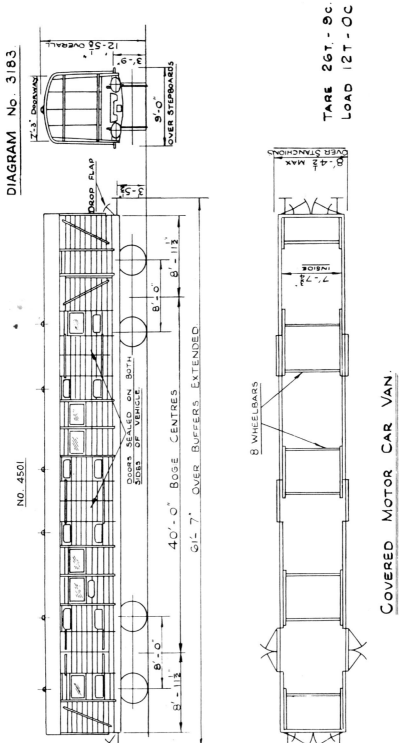

DIAGRAM No. 3183

12·58" OVERALL

2'-3" DOORWAY

3'-9"

9'-0"
OVER STEPBOARDS

TARE 26T - 9c.
LOAD 12T - 0C

DROP FLAP

NO. 4501

8'-0"

8' - 11½"

DOORS SEALED ON BOTH
SIDES OF VEHICLE.

40'-0" BOGIE CENTRES

61'-7" OVER BUFFERS EXTENDED.

8'-0"

8' - 11½"

8' - 11½"

8'-4½" MAX.
OVER STANCHIONS

INSIDE
7'-7¾"

8 WHEELBARS

COVERED MOTOR CAR VAN.

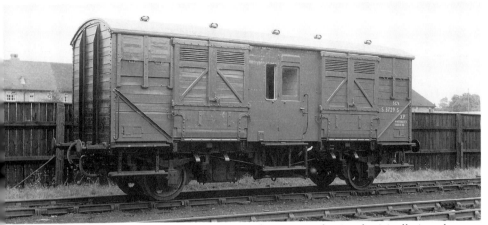

Special cattle van No. 3729, built in September 1952, and painted originally in red livery with black ends and underframe. It is fitted with vacuum brakes and electric lighting. Note handbrake lever underneath door. *Courtesy National Railway Museum*

Steam-heating boiler van No. TDS 70191 at Oxford, 29th April, 1975. It was rebuilt from special cattle van No. 3703 in December 1962. *H.C. Casserley*

One of the bogie luggage vans, No. 2291, was reconstructed as a motor car van and placed on the underframe of corridor brake composite No. 6897 in 1960. In this picture, taken at Clapham Junction on 17th May, 1961, the lengthened bodywork is at the left-hand end. No. 4501 also has doors in the ends for vehicle access. *D. Cullum*

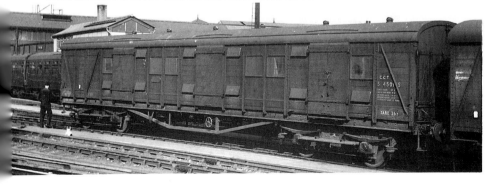

eight wheelbars to prevent the motor vehicles from movement. The SR 8 ft-wheelbase bogies were retained and bogie centres measured 40 ft. Buckeye automatic couplings also were retained. No. 4501 (Diagram No. 3183) left Eastleigh Works in September 1960.

On a trial run from Margate to Sidmouth the van carried a maximum of four small cars, and later the wheelbars inside the van were altered so that more vehicles could be squeezed in. However, the van was so non-standard that its life as a car-carrier was extremely short, and by 1964 the vehicle was being shown in lists as a general utility van. In March 1966 it was withdrawn from service.

SPECIAL CATTLE VANS
Summary of Building and Withdrawal Dates

Built		Withdrawn	Built		Withdrawn
3679	6.30	9.61	3710	7.30	12.62
3680	6.30	3.63	1	7.30	12.62
1	6.30	12.62	2	7.30	5.61
2	6.30	12.62	3	7.30 Body sold from	4.63
3	6.30	12.62		Inverurie	
4	6.30	12.62	4	7.30	12.62
5	6.30	2.62	5	7.30	12.62
6	6.30	12.62	6	7.30 To DS70190,	c.9.88
7	6.30	10.62		62	
8	6.30	12.62	7	7.30	12.62
9	6.30	12.62	8	7.30	12.62
3690	6.30	12.62	9	7.30	5.61
1	6.30 Body sold from	10.63	3720	7.30	12.62
	Inverurie		1	7.30	12.62
2	6.30	12.62	2	7.30	12.62
3	6.30	12.62	3	7.30	12.62
4	6.30	12.62	4	7.30 Body sold from	11.63
5	6.30	12.62		Inverurie	
6	6.30	12.62	5	7.30 Body sold from	9.63
7	6.30	12.62		Inverurie	
8	6.30	4.61	6	7.30	12.62
9	6.30	12.62	7	7.30	12.62
3700	6.30	12.62	8	7.30	12.62
1	6.30	7.62	9	9.52	12.70
2	6.30	8.62	3730	9.52	12.70
3	6.30 To DS70191,	3.82	1	9.52	9.68
	12.62		2	9.52	12.70
4	6.30	12.62	3	9.52	12.71
5	6.30 Body sold from	4.63	4	9.52	9.67
	Inverurie		5	9.52	5.66
6	6.30	12.62	6	9.52	10.71
7	6.30	4.61	7	10.52	8.68
8	6.30	12.62	3738	9.52	10.66
9	7.30 Body sold from	7.63			
	Inverurie				

Chapter Nine
Milk Tanks

A very important traffic on all the railways for many years was milk. By 1927, over 280 million gallons of milk per year were being carried. The liquid was loaded into metal churns, which were placed in specially-designed milk vans; these had slatted sides so that when the train was in motion the inrush of air kept the churns cool. It was absolutely essential that milk be conveyed without delay from the dairies to the bottling plants in and around London; the trains left the country depots every evening and would arrive in London in the small hours. Stations such as Vauxhall, destination of milk trains since at least 1910, would echo to the crash and rumble of the churns as they were skilfully rolled along the platform by porters. In the afternoon the empty churns were worked back to the country depots again and so the daily cycle went on.

And then someone hit on the bright idea of carrying the milk in tanks mounted on ordinary wagon underframes. It was reckoned that each tank, which could hold 3,000 gallons, carried the equivalent of three vans of churns – a considerable reduction in deadweight.

The Great Western and the London, Midland & Scottish Railway Companies were the first to build wagon frames to carry fixed tanks owned by United Dairies Ltd and a service was inaugurated on 1st December, 1927, from Wootton Bassett (GW) and Calveley (LMS) to Mitre Bridge, Willesden.

These early tanks were of steel, lined with glass enamel fused into the steel at such a high temperature that it could never crack. Next came an insulating layer of cork and finally the outer steel shell. It was stated that even on the hottest day the milk would not increase its temperature by more than one degree.

Compressed air was used to discharge the milk from the tanks, which, when empty, were rinsed with cold water, scrubbed, rinsed in hot water and finally sterilised with high-pressure steam. Every trace of milk had to be eliminated before the tanks were returned empty to the dairy.

The Southern Railway was still carrying all its milk in churns when the London & North Eastern Railway, in September 1928, introduced glass-lined tanks for United Dairies traffic. Three years later a typical Southern milk train from Dorset to Vauxhall, starting its journey with five vans loaded with 253 churns, included a bogie luggage van, a 6-wheeled van, an aeroplane van and one of the latest gangwayed bogie luggage vans conveying 142 churns. Twelve more vans were added during the journey, plus a further 12 at Salisbury, and these contained churns for Margate, Sydenham, Lewisham and Victoria, detached at Clapham Junction. Leaving Salisbury the load was 800 tons or 22,700 gallons.

In the year ended June 1931 the SR carried 27,684,202 gallons in 1,977,443 churns to London; most of the loads coming from Gillingham (Dorset), Templecombe, Semley and Salisbury. All these places were on the old South Western main line, but the 'Brighton' had a look-in too, for nearly 71,000 churns were loaded at Billingshurst. At Vauxhall the churns were transported between platform and ground level by lifts.

The first 4-wheel truck built by Lancing in September 1931 for the purpose of carrying CWS mobile milk tank trailers. This picture shows No. 4401, with a Dyson trailer secured by eight binding chains. *W.O. Steel Collection*

CWS mobile tank trailer being hauled on to an SR truck, probably at Cole. Note the wire rope and pulleys and the flanged runways to guide the road wheels of the trailer. *W.O. Steel Collection*

If the Southern was the last of the companies to introduce bulk conveyance of milk by rail, at least it was the first to use wagons designed for carrying road milk tank trailers. In September 1931 Lancing Works constructed three 4-wheeled trucks, 21 ft 6 in. over headstocks (the underframes conforming to those used in Railway Clearing House 20-ton mineral wagons) to Order No. 661, Diagram 3151. They were numbered 4401–3 and, as they were for use in passenger-rated trains, they had vacuum brakes as well as hand brakes and were through-piped for steam heating. They could and did run in ordinary passenger trains.

The tank trailers, of which there were two (a third being added in 1932), were built by R.A. Dyson & Co. of Liverpool and were the property of the Co-operative Wholesale Society. Capacity of the glass-lined Butler tank was 2,000 gallons, or as much as 200 churns. Because of weight restrictions on the road, and loading gauge restrictions on the railway, capacity of the mobile tanks could not be as high as the fixed tanks. Each tank was lettered 'Pure New Milk. Co-operative Wholesale Society Ltd. Milk Department London.'

On the road the trailers ran on 6-wheeled chassis with solid tyres and the front pair had Ackerman steering operated from a tiller bar to which the drawbar was attached. Hauled from the dairy to Cole Station (Somerset & Dorset Joint) the tank trailer was then hauled on to the railway truck by a motor tractor using a wire rope and pulleys fitted to each end of the truck. The wagon had end flaps so that the trailer could be run on from a loading dock, and the floor had flanged runways to guide the road wheels of the trailer. Wheel chocks were formed into position by adjustable wedges; the trailer was then secured by eight stout binding chains with screw adjustment. On the road the trailers were rather squat in appearance but once mounted on a rail wagon they looked 'high-and-dry'.

This new CWS service from Cole to Clapham Junction was introduced in October 1931. At Clapham Junction the truck, still with its tank, was shunted alongside the CWS depot adjacent to the station where the milk was discharged, the tank cleaned in the same way as a fixed tank, and then returned empty to Cole where the trailer would be offloaded and run by road to the dairy again.

The Southern also introduced its first fixed milk tank wagons later that year. Six 4-wheeled underframes, 21 ft 6 in. over headstocks, were built at Lancing in October and November 1931 to Order No. 673, Diagram 3152, for United Dairies glass-lined 3,000-gal. tanks. The wagons were numbered 4404–9 and were soon formed in the 6.5 pm milk train from Sherborne to Waterloo. Tanks were white with black lettering and solebars were black with white lettering.

Using 4-wheeled frames was soon found to be a mistake. Riding was unsteady at high speeds and the milk tended to slosh about, with some risk of its turning to butter. For all future construction the Board of Trade required that 6-wheeled frames be used, the thinking being that if a 6-wheeled locomotive tender full of water could ride well then so should a 6-wheeled milk tank. Restrictions were drawn up by the SR for the running of

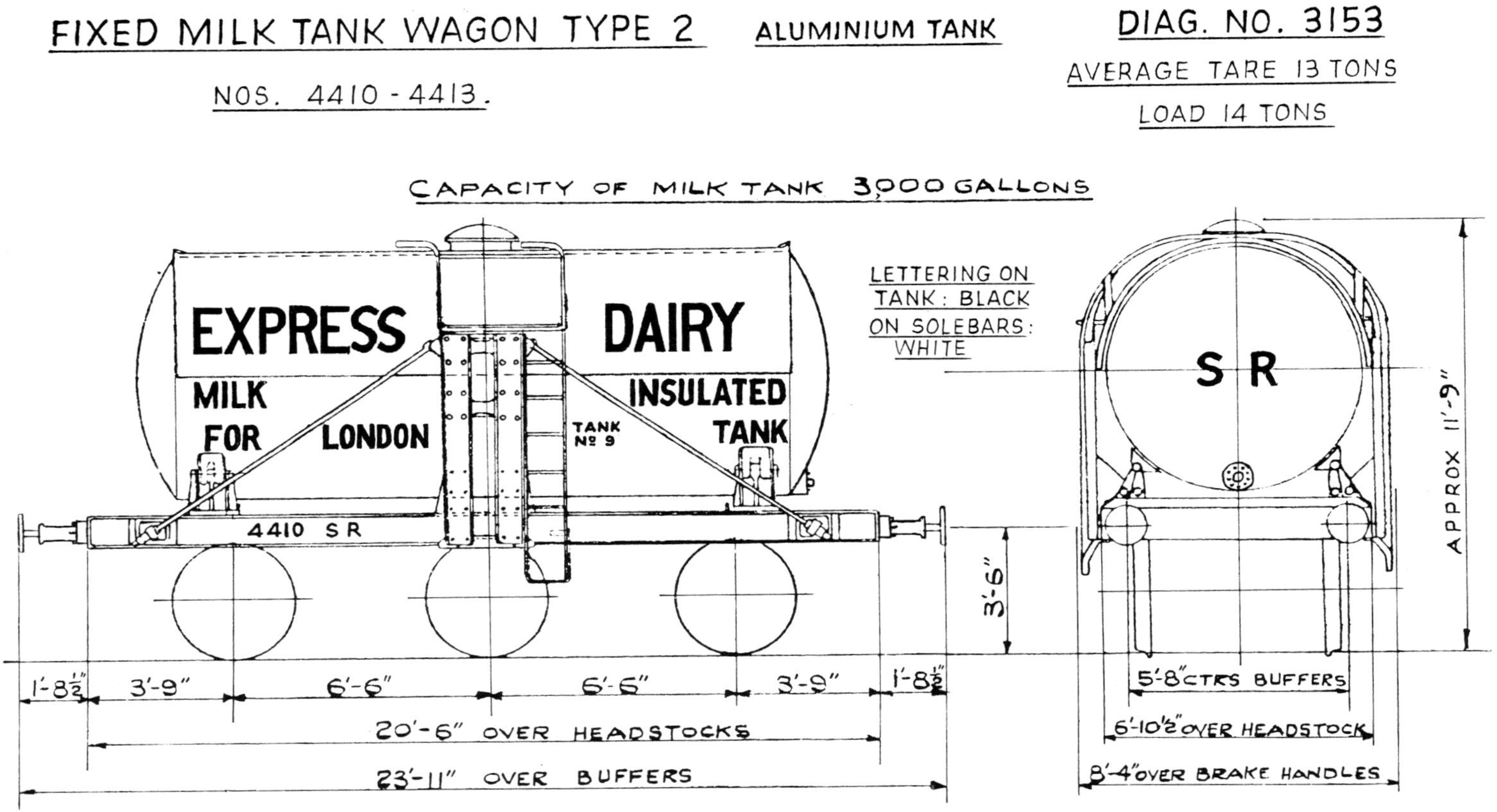

FIXED MILK TANK WAGON TYPE 2 — ALUMINIUM TANK

DIAG. NO. 3153

AVERAGE TARE 13 TONS

LOAD 14 TONS

NOS. 4410 - 4413.

CAPACITY OF MILK TANK 3,000 GALLONS

LETTERING ON TANK: BLACK
ON SOLEBARS: WHITE

APPROX 11'-9"

S R

S R

5'-8"CTRS BUFFERS

6'-10½" OVER HEADSTOCK

8'-4" OVER BRAKE HANDLES

DAIRY

INSULATED TANK

TANK No 9

EXPRESS

MILK FOR LONDON

4410 S R

3'-6"

1'-8½"

3'-9"

6'-6"

6'-6"

3'-9"

1'-8½"

20'-6" OVER HEADSTOCKS

23'-11" OVER BUFFERS

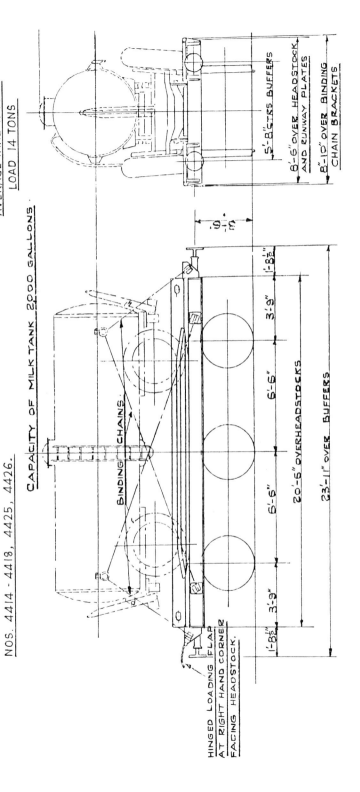

MOBILE TANK CARRIAGE TRUCK TYPE 2

NOS. 4414 - 4418, 4425, 4426.

CAPACITY OF MILK TANK 2000 GALLONS.

DIAG. NO. 3154

AVERAGE TARE II TONS

LOAD 14 TONS

5'-8⅝" B'CK'RS BUFFERS

8'-6" OVER HEADSTOCK AND RUNWAY PLATES

8'-10" OVER BINDING CHAIN BRACKETS

2'-6"

BINDING CHAINS.

HINGED LOADING FLAP AT RIGHT HAND CORNER FACING HEADSTOCK.

1'-8½"   3'-9"   6'-6"   6'-6"   3'-9"   1'-8½"

20'-6" OVER HEADSTOCKS

23'-11" OVER BUFFERS

Three 6-wheeled trucks (Diagram 3154), including part of No. 4417, at Salisbury; two Dyson 2,000-gal. mobile milk tanks belonging to United Dairies.

M.S. King Collection

Mobile milk tank carrier No. 4425, built at Lancing in February 1933. It was withdrawn in 1961. Maiden Newton, 20th September, 1952. *A.E. West*

4-wheeled tanks and mobile tanks loaded on 4-wheeled trucks:

If run in passenger trains they must not be formed between vehicles conveying passengers.

If formed in trains which exceed a speed of 40 miles per hour at any point they must not be attached to the rear without a six- or eight-wheeled vehicle, or a four-wheeled vehicle having a wheelbase of not less than 15 feet, being attached immediately behind.

Four-wheeled milk tanks and mobile milk tanks loaded on four-wheeled trucks may be formed in any position in non-passenger trains which do not exceed a speed of 40 miles per hour.

The first 6-wheeled frames were built at Lancing in May and June 1932 for Express Dairy fixed tank wagons. The four frames were 20 ft 6 in. over headstocks, vacuum braked and piped for steam heating: Order No. 697, Diagram 3153, vehicle Nos. 4410–3. The tanks were aluminium and loaded 14 tons, or 3,000 gallons.

Lancing also built, in June and August 1932, five 6-wheeled trucks for United Dairies mobile tanks: they were 20 ft 6 in. over headstocks, to Order No. 698, Diagram 3154, vehicle Nos. 4414–8. The Dyson trailers each had a 2,000-gal. stainless steel tank made by Thompson Bros of Bilston and differed from the CWS trailers in having only four wheels, with Dunlop giant low-pressure pneumatic tyres mounted on Dyson's patent drum-wheel system, instead of six wheels with solid tyres. The drum-wheel system was designed to guide the trailer into its correct position on the rail wagon and to take the weight off the tyres during rail transit. The drum-wheels engaged with a guiding plate and elevating rail on the wagon; as the trailer was pulled into position the weight was taken off the tyres and transferred to the drum-wheels. Loading and securing the trailer was carried out generally as for the CWS ones.

The tanks were of Firth's 'Staybrite' stainless steel, ⅛-in. thick, insulated with six layers of 'Alfol' and covered with 18-gauge aluminium, painted dark grey externally.

. The wagons were fitted with elevated tracks, the centre portions of which were level and the ends downward-sloping. There were hinged flaps at each end of the wagon for end loading and unloading of the trailers.

These UD trailers were put into service between Gillingham (Dorset), Salisbury and Forest Hill. Two further wagons to carry UD Dyson trailers, Nos. 4425/6, were built at Lancing in February 1933 (Order No. 739, Diagram 3154). In that year a demonstration of loading the trailer on to the wagon, using a motor tractor and wire rope and pulleys, was given at Forest Hill station. However, no more trucks for mobile tanks were built; all further construction was of fixed tanks only.

In October 1932 Lancing turned out six 6-wheeled trucks for United Dairies 3,000-gallon glass-lined tanks: Order No. L721, Diagram 3155, 20 ft 6 in. over headstocks, Nos. 4419–24. They were followed in May 1933 by two for Express Dairies 3,000-gal. stainless steel tanks: Order No. 747, Diagram 3156, Nos. 4427-8. A further four for United Dairies came out of Lancing in September 1933 (Order No. 768, Diagram 3157, Nos. 4429–32). These tanks were glass-lined.

FIXED MILK TANK WAGON TYPE 3 GLASS LINED   DIAG. NO. 3155

AVERAGE TARE 15 TONS
LOAD 14 TONS

NOS. 4419 - 4424.

CAPACITY OF MILK TANK 3,000 GALLONS

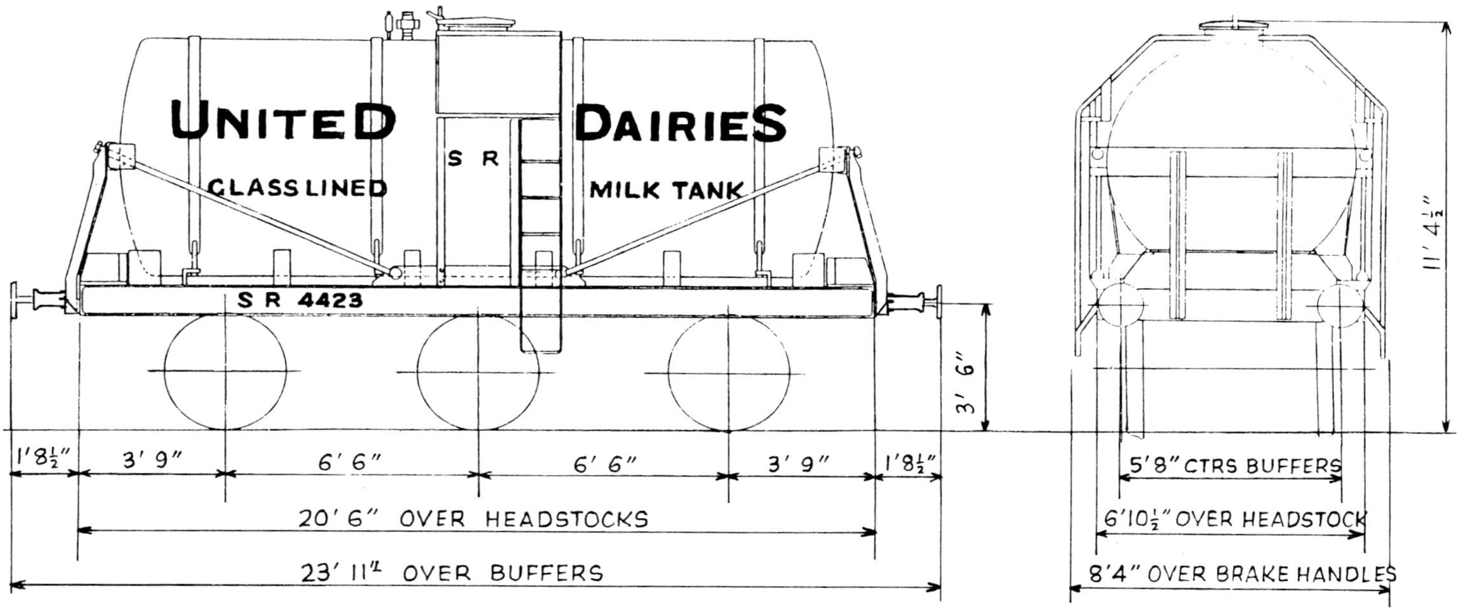

11' 4½"

5' 8" CTRS BUFFERS

6' 10½" OVER HEADSTOCK

8' 4" OVER BRAKE HANDLES

3' 6"

1' 8½"

3' 9"

6' 6"

6' 6"

3' 9"

1' 8½"

20' 6" OVER HEADSTOCKS

23' 11¼" OVER BUFFERS

UNITED DAIRIES

GLASS LINED

MILK TANK

S R

S R 4423

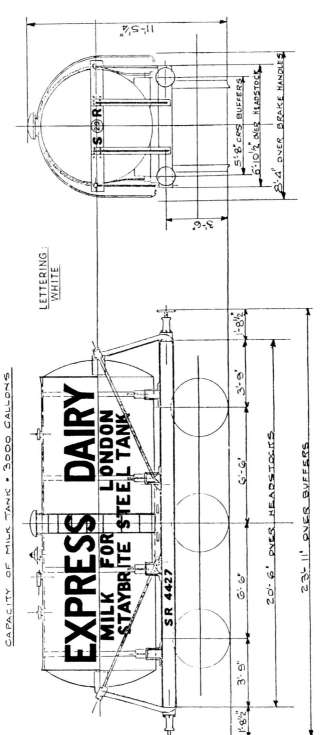

FIXED MILK TANK WAGON TYPE 4   STAINLESS STEEL TANK   DIAG. NO. 3156

NOS. 4427, 4428.

AVERAGE TARE 12 TONS

LOAD 14 TONS

CAPACITY OF MILK TANK - 3000 GALLONS

LETTERING:
WHITE

EXPRESS DAIRY
MILK FOR LONDON
STAYBRITE STEEL TANK

SR 4427

S 29 R

11'-5¼"

5'-8" CRS BUFFERS
6'-10½" OVER HEADSTOCK
8'-4" OVER BRAKE HANDLES

3'-6"

1'-8½"
3'-9"
6'-6"
6'-6"
3'-9"
1'-8½"

20'-6' OVER HEADSTOCKS

23'-11" OVER BUFFERS

Two views of fixed milk tank wagon No. 4408, built at Lancing in November 1931. The tank, which was the property of the dairy, carried 3,000 gallons. The underframe was owned by the railway.   *Courtesy H.M.R.S.*

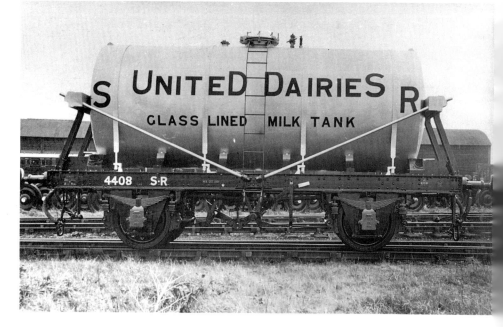

Express Dairy fixed tank on SR wagon No. 4410 (incorrectly lettered '4401'). No. 4410 (Diagram 3153) was built at Lancing in May 1932. *M.S. King Collection*

Express Dairy steel tank on SR wagon No. 4427 (Diagram 3156), built at Lancing in May 1933. *G. Bixley Collection*

The next order was for two trucks, Nos.4433–4, which Ashford Works built in April 1935. These, Order No. 828 to Diagram 3158, were built for West Park Dairy but this concern was amalgamated with Express Dairies before the wagons were completed. Consequently the 3,000-gal. glass-lined tanks never wore the West Park livery of cream with chocolate lettering.

These small batches of tanks, for different dairies, were very similar in appearance but no decision seemed to be made as to the best material to use: aluminium, stainless steel or glass enamel. In later years stainless steel was favoured for its high resistance to the corrosive action of milk (which could seriously affect some metals) and the ease with which it could be cleaned and sterilised.

In 1937 came a decision to withdraw the original nine 4-wheeled trucks of 1931 and use them for new 20-ton mineral wagons, which received the numbers 41201–9 – though not necessarily in the same order. Six new 6-wheeled frames were built at Ashford in 1937 for Nos. 4404–9 and three in 1938 with the intention of using them with the CWS Dyson 6-wheeled trailers (Order No. 938, Diagram Nos. 3159 and 3160). The original UD glass-lined tanks were mounted on the new frames 4404–9; but there is some doubt as to whether the other three 6-wheeled frames were ever used by CWS. Nos. 4401–3 do not show up in any post-War lists, nor does CWS feature in any wartime or post-War milk traffic on the Southern Railway, and it could be that the contract with CWS was not renewed in 1938. CWS trailers were still worked onto the SR, but mounted on GWR trucks.

A large number of new 6-wheeled trucks, to Diagram 3161, was built for use by Express Dairies stainless steel 3,000-gal. tanks. Nos. 4435–8 (Order No. 986) were built at Ashford in 1937/8; Nos. 4439–42 (Order No. 1750) in 1942; and Nos. 4443–54 (E2600) at Eastleigh in 1943/4. This last batch was built for the Ministry of Transport and did not come into railway ownership until December 1951.

Finally, a further 12 frames to Diagram 3157 were constructed for United Dairies' use (3,000-gal. glass-lined tanks) which also were the property of the MOT until December 1951. Nos. 4455–60 (Order No. L2630) were built at Lancing in 1943/4 and Nos. 4461–6 (Order No. E3040) at Eastleigh in 1944.

Working of Milk Tanks

Workings of vans in passenger trains were precisely laid down but milk tanks were operated more like goods wagons and the number formed in any given train could vary from day to day. In the Working Notice for May 1936, for example, the following trains included an unspecified number of milk tanks:

11.25 am Semley to Waterloo.
8.44 pm (SO), 9.11 pm (SX) Clapham Junction to Waterloo.
3.08 am Waterloo to Semley.
9.48 pm Waterloo to Salisbury. Also 1 tank (SX) for Seaton Junction and 1 tank (SX) for Cricklade.
4.42 am Clapham Junction to Salisbury.

FIXED MILK TANK WAGON TYPE 5   GLASS LINED   DIAG. NO. 3157

AVERAGE TARE 14 TONS
LOAD 14 TONS

NOS. 4429 - 4432, 4455 - 4466.

CAPACITY OF MILK TANK 3,000 GALLONS

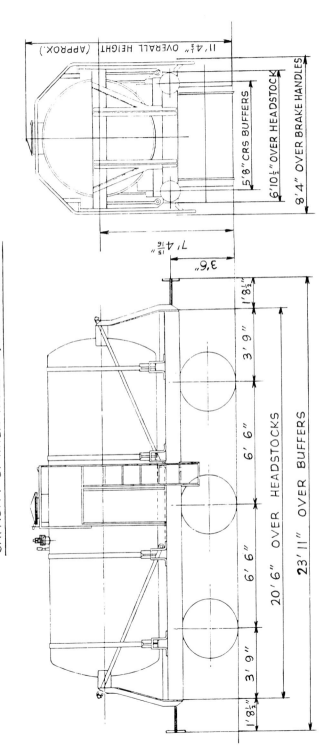

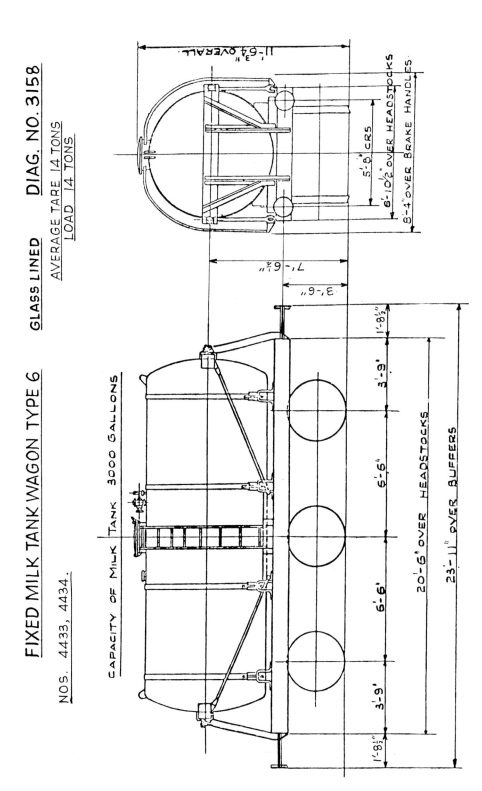

FIXED MILK TANK WAGON TYPE 6 GLASS LINED DIAG. NO. 3158

NOS. 4433, 4434.

AVERAGE TARE 14 TONS
LOAD 14 TONS

CAPACITY OF MILK TANK 3000 GALLONS

11'-6¾" OVERALL

5'-8" CRS
6'-10½" OVER HEADSTOCKS
8'-4" OVER BRAKE HANDLES

7'-6½"
3'-6"

1'-8½"
3'-9'
6'-6"
6'-6"
3'-9'
1'-8½"
20'-6' OVER HEADSTOCKS
23'-11" OVER BUFFERS

FIXED MILK TANK WAGON TYPE I CONVERTED GLASS LINED DIAG NO. 3159

AVERAGE TARE 14 TONS

LOAD 14 TONS

NOS. 4404 - 4409.

CAPACITY OF MILK TANK 3,000 GALLONS

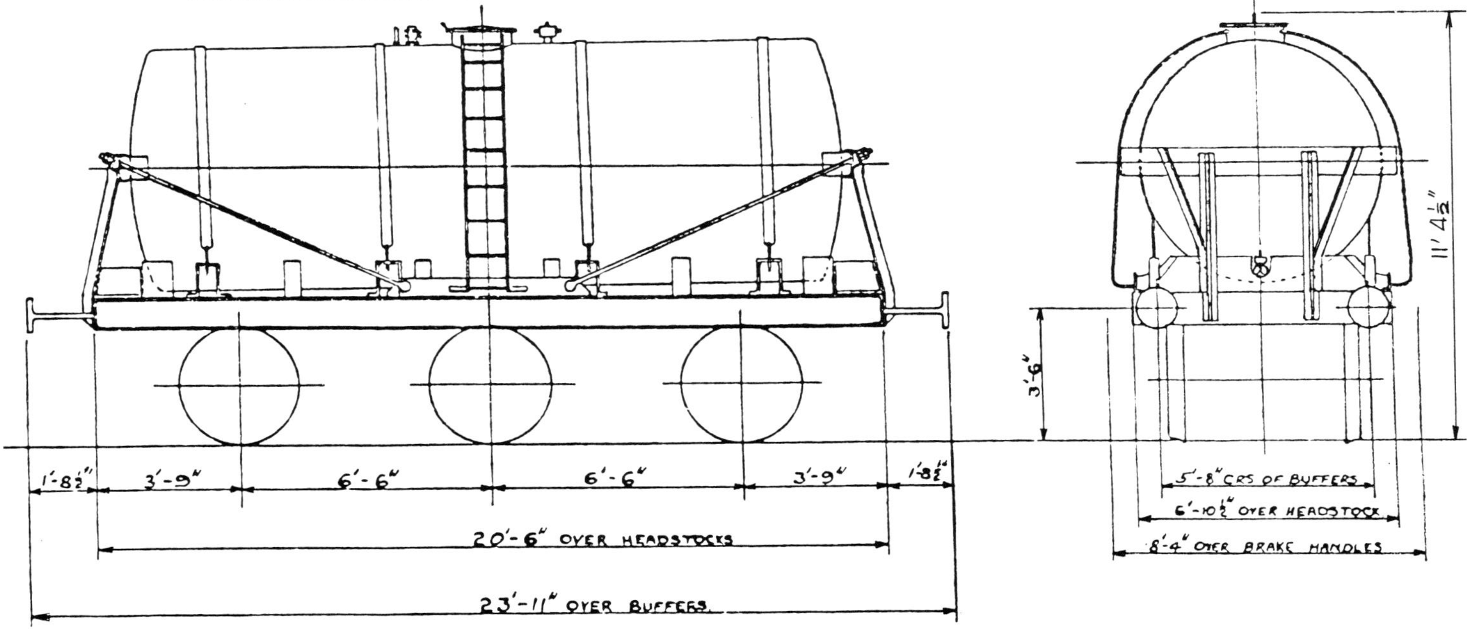

11' 4½"

5'-8" CRS OF BUFFERS

6'-10½" OVER HEADSTOCK

8'-4" OVER BRAKE HANDLES

3'-6"

1'-8½"

3'-9"

6'-6"

6'-6"

3'-9"

1'-8½"

20'-6" OVER HEADSTOCKS

23'-11" OVER BUFFERS

MOBILE TANK CARRIAGE TRUCK

NOS. 4401 - 4403.

DIAG. NO. 3160

AVERAGE TARE - TONS

LOAD 15 TONS

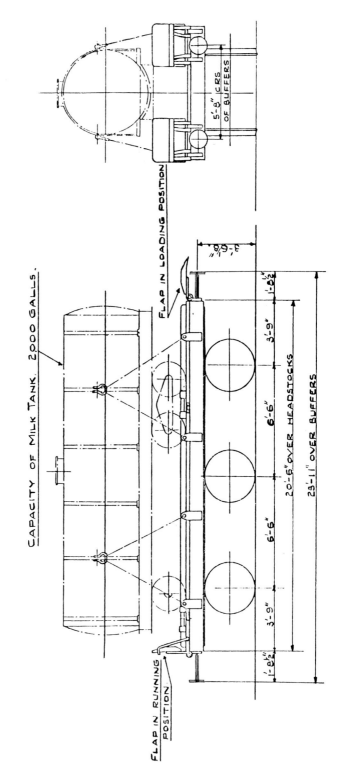

CAPACITY OF MILK TANK. 2000 GALLS.

FLAP IN LOADING POSITION

FLAP IN RUNNING POSITION

5'-8" CRS OF BUFFERS

3'-1"

1'-2"

3'-9"

6'-6"

6'-6"

3'-9"

1'-2"

20'-6" OVER HEADSTOCKS

23'-11" OVER BUFFERS

FIXED MILK TANK WAGON TYPE 7 <u>STAINLESS STEEL</u>

<u>DIAG. NO. 3161</u>

<u>AVERAGE TARE 14 TONS</u>

<u>LOAD 14 TONS</u>

<u>NOS. 4435 – 4454.</u>

<u>CAPACITY OF MILK TANK 3,000 GALLONS</u>

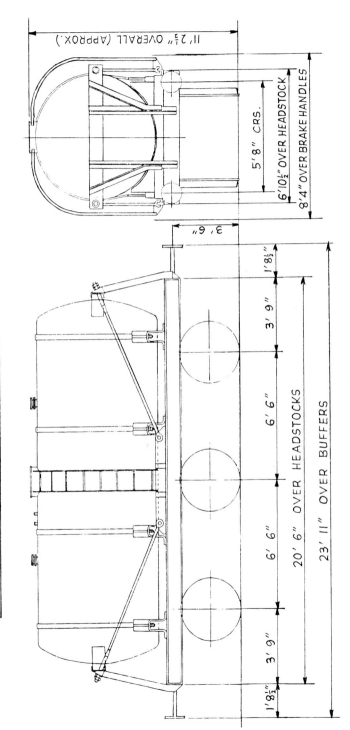

In addition, 2 tanks were formed in the 3.45 am Waterloo to Petersfield, 1 tank (SO) in the 6.00 pm Waterloo to Exeter, and 1 tank for Cricklade left Clapham Junction at 3.58 pm.

Sunday workings were entirely different. Leaving Waterloo, the 3.35 am to Portsmouth Harbour included 2 tanks for Petersfield, the 11.00 am had one for Salisbury, and the 2.12 pm had one for Cricklade and one for Seaton Junction. Leaving Clapham Junction the 6.00 am had tanks for Semley and Salisbury, the 5.04 pm for Waterloo had one and the 9.12 pm for Waterloo an unspecified number. These trains still included many vans for milk in churns as this traffic could not be replaced overnight.

Vauxhall depot by January 1933 was achieving 1 million gallons per month. The station was remodelled in 1935 with eight platforms and all had conduits to the creamery. Milk trains always stood on the Up Windsor slow line for unloading; when this work was completed they continued to Waterloo for reversal and worked back to Clapham Junction empty. By 1938 Vauxhall was dealing with 34,000 gallons per day; pipe lines under all eight tracks led direct to the bottling plant, which was across the station approach on the down side.

The West of England depots were at Torrington, Lapford, Crediton, Seaton Junction, Chard Junction, Yeovil and Semley. Even in 1939 the milk tanks at Semley were, like as not, still being shunted by horse!

It was to be many years before the conveyance of milk in churns ceased. By 1941 there was a daily milk train from Yeovil to Tonbridge, detached from the main train at Woking and worked via Guildford and Redhill, due at Tonbridge at 2.45 am. The empty churns returned on the 9.00 pm van train from Tonbridge to Woking. By 1949 this milk train was leaving Yeovil at 5.40 pm and running through to Gravesend via Tonbridge and Maidstone West daily. Return from Gravesend was at 2.40 pm (SX), 3.58 pm (SO), 4.00 pm Sundays. It was discontinued in 1956, but 10 years later CWS churns were still being forwarded by rail from Stewarts Lane to Kent Coast destinations.

West of England milk workings had been reorganised by 1946 and there were more Clapham Junction to Waterloo runs. There were departures at 2.30 am daily, 7.55 am Sundays, 9.57 am weekdays, 9.20 pm weekdays and 9.35 pm Sundays, all these being booked to stand at Vauxhall for 3–4 hours for unloading. The 3.54 pm Clapham Junction to Exmouth Junction milk empties (2.24 pm on Sundays) ran at that time for many years.

The 1949 workings were similar. The 5.18 pm Sidmouth Junction to Waterloo tanks (due 3.44 am) had the following instruction in the Working Timetable: 'Milk Tanks for Wimbledon will be detached at Wimbledon. Woking to attach van behind Tanks. Load from Woking not to exceed 96 wheels plus traffic detached at Wimbledon'. One had visions of the staff at Woking feverishly counting all the wheels in the dark; but they must have found a simpler way of estimating the load. Another tank train was the 9.05 pm Templecombe to Clapham Junction via East Putney, due 12.20 am.

In 1954 Express Dairies opened a new bottling plant at Morden South, on the Wimbledon–Sutton line. Milk tank trains worked there from Clapham Junction, but as there was no runround for the locomotive the trains, after unloading, had to continue to the next station, St Helier, reversing there and returning empty to Clapham Junction. The Morden South plant had its own locomotive, a 4-wheeled Ruston & Hornsby diesel No. 235511 of 1945; it was later replaced by a Hunslet 4-wheeled diesel locomotive *David*, No. 5308 of 1960. This had fallen out of use by February 1979.

Much of the traffic for Morden South came off the Western Region via Kensington and in later years it all did. Milk train workings in 1961 and 1962 from Clapham Junction to Morden South were: 2.30 and 4.05 am (on Sundays, 2.55, 4.30 and 6.53 am) and from Morden South to Clapham Junction empties at 3.05 am, 1.07 pm (SX), 1.01 pm (SO) and 12.45 pm on Sundays. A train timed at 10.04 am from Clapham Junction ran if required.

Decline of milk traffic by rail began after the locomen's strike of 1955, during which the dairies were forced to find other means of transporting the milk. Having found it some of them stuck to it and did not return to the railway when the strike was over. The first withdrawals of milk tanks came in 1959, when four examples of Diagram 3161 were condemned (No. 4452 had already been withdrawn in 1955). The road/rail trade collapsed around 1960, and the mobile tank carriers Nos. 4414–8/25/6 were condemned, although not officially withdrawn until June 1961. Road tankers were now used to take the milk direct from dairy to bottling plant; where the dairy was rail-connected, however, good use was still being made of the railway for transporting milk.

The West of England tank workings in 1955 were as follows:

5.36 pm Crediton to Exeter Central. This detached at least 1 tank at Exeter St David's for attachment to the Penzance–Paddington service.

4.00 pm Lapford to Exeter Central.

6.48 pm Perishables Exeter Central to Waterloo. Included tanks from Crediton and Lapford as detailed above.

9.05 pm Templecombe to Clapham Junction tanks attached to 6.48 pm from Exeter. Maximum load leaving Templecombe 23 tanks plus Van B-723 tons.

8.11 pm Yeovil Junction to Clapham Junction tanks attached to 6.48 pm from Exeter.

Any tanks off the S&DJ line were to go forward from Templecombe at 9.05 pm.

3.54 pm empty tanks Clapham Junction to Exeter Central.

The 1960 workings were similar, but by June 1962 the Exeter Central to Clapham Junction train was leaving at 7.36 pm; some tanks were attached to the 5.30 pm Exeter Central to Salisbury stopping train, probably at Semley, and transferred to the 7.36 pm from Exeter, which left Salisbury at 9.55 pm. Next morning at 9.26 am the tanks left for Vauxhall, where four hours were allowed for unloading and cleaning. A 'West Country' Pacific (Exmouth Junction depot) then took the tanks to Waterloo, ran round them in the sidings on the north side and returned with them to Clapham Junction at 2.10 pm. Here further tanks as required were added, as well as a few vans, and at 3.54 pm the train left for Exeter Central via East Putney and Wimbledon. The load varied from day to day.

The whole of the milk traffic along the former South Western main line ceased at the time that line was reduced in status: from 7th September, 1964.

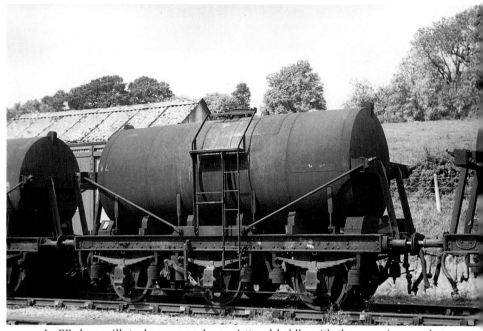

In BR days milk tanks were no longer lettered boldly with the owner's name but merely bore a plate on the right-hand part of the tank, which was seldom cleaned externally. Here is No. 4422 (built at Lancing in October 1932), a United Dairies tank at Hemyock, WR, on 24th August, 1963. *P.H. Swift*

Express Dairy tank (SR No. 4427, built at Lancing in May 1933) here looks fairly clean but the small label is unimpressive when compared with the original style of lettering. Seaton Junction, 5th September, 1964. *A.E. West*

A Sunday train survived until 1965. These were the changes that resulted in the loss of the 'Atlantic Coast Express', the end of through trains beyond Exeter and of local trains and finally, in 1967, the singling of most of the line between Salisbury and Exeter.

Milk traffic was now concentrated along the Western Region main line, the tanks coming on to the Southern over the West London line. The SR tanks – of which several still remained – were mixed in with WR ones. As they all looked very similar, and as all were coated externally with a layer of dirt, it was hard for the observer to differentiate between them. Exceptionally, Express Dairies' tanks were kept in superb condition until the late 1950s.

There had always been extensive milk traffic over the WL line, and Kensington Olympia was an important sorting point. In 1949 tanks were run from Kensington to Victoria, Stewarts Lane and East Croydon. By 1956 there were workings from Kensington to Stewarts Lane at 2.45 am (MX), 3.05 am (MO), 3.55 am (SO), 6.40 am and 1.30 pm (SX), 1.40 pm (SO). From Clapham Junction tanks worked at 1.25 am to Victoria on Mondays and Stewarts Lane (MX), and at 11.50 pm to Victoria. Tanks were returned from Stewarts Lane to Kensington at 12.45 pm. There were also workings from Clapham Junction to Mottingham (on the Dartford Loop line) at 2.35 am and to Holborn Viaduct at 6.45 pm (SO). The Mottingham depot had been installed by 1947 for Express Dairies and milk tank trains ran there daily until the early 1960s.

By June 1966 there were just two trains from Kensington to Stewarts Lane each day and these were maintained until about 1972; from May 1972 only one working of tanks was shown from Clapham Yard to Stewarts Lane and back, these tanks having been detached from the 3.08 am ex Acton. Even this working had ceased by May 1973.

Tanks for Vauxhall depot now worked via Kensington and the men working these trips knew them as the 'Kenny Tanks'. Weekday workings for 1969 left Clapham Junction for Vauxhall at 1.30 (MX), 2.30 (MO) and 9.36 am; but by 1972 only the 9.36 remained. This arrived at Waterloo (Platform 15) at 1.15 pm, returning for Clapham Junction 20 minutes later. Departure for Acton was at 3.09 pm.

By 1973 there was often only one tank from St Erth to Vauxhall each day, and it was worked from Clapham Junction (coupled to a brake van) by a class '09' diesel shunter. On one occasion in 1976 this tiny train was worked by one of the big class '74' electro-diesel locomotives. At Vauxhall the tanks were connected by flexible hoses to discharge the milk through pipes from the platform, passing under the road outside the station to the bottling depot. During this operation the up Windsor line trains had to use the Up Through line platform. The Vauxhall workings ceased around 1976/7.

The Morden South tanks continued for a couple more years. The 1967 workings were: 6.40 pm Tiverton Junction to Morden South and 3.45 am (MX), 4.15 (MO), Kensington to Morden South, all returning on the 1.07 pm freight to Wimbledon, thence Clapham Junction. The May 1972 workings were: 1.12 am Acton to Clapham Junction, 2.25 am Clapham Junction to Morden South, 1.07 pm Morden South to Clapham Junction and 3.09 pm

Clapham Junction to Acton (which also included the tanks from Vauxhall). By 1975 it needed only one train from Acton to Clapham Junction, the 2.08 am, to include the tanks for both Vauxhall and Morden South, and by 1979 the Morden South service had ceased.

All that remained from May 1979 was a train leaving St Erth at 4.42 pm for Clapham Yard (due 4.27 am MX), returning at 3.44 pm for Acton. On Sundays the train left Penzance at 2.00 pm, due Clapham Yard at 2.35 am on Mondays. After this service finished in October 1979 there was no longer any milk traffic on the Southern. Most of the Southern tanks had been withdrawn by 1976 but 14 remained after that date, and they survived till the end of milk trains on the Southern.

In 1974 Nos. 4433/4 were transferred to departmental service and converted into water carriers for use in emergency at Severn Tunnel Junction on the Western Region. No. 4433 was renumbered TDB 975452 but No. 4434 merely became DS 4434.

Only two tanks have been preserved. No. 4409 was acquired by the Great Western Society at Didcot, and No. 4430 was obtained by the Bluebell Railway in August 1981 following its withdrawal in 1980. The actual tank was donated by St Ivel, but the underframe, being BR property, had to be *bought* by the Bluebell!

The Bluebell Railway owns United Dairies milk tank No. 4430 (built at Lancing in September 1933) and occasionally runs it in passenger trains for visual effect. On 10th May, 1987, it was at the front of the 2.35 pm from Sheffield Park to Horsted Keynes.   *Author*

MILK TANKS
Summary of Building and Withdrawal Dates

Built		Withdrawn	Built		Withdrawn
4401	9.31 *	12.38	4436	12.37	73
2	9.31 *	12.38	7	1.38	c.78
3	9.31 *	12.38	8	3.38	6.63
4	10.31 New frame 11.37	76	9	1942	73
5	10.31 New frame 12.37	74	4440	1942	73
6	10.31 New frame 9.37	c.77	1	1942	76
7	10.31 New frame 8.37	c.77	2	1942	c.78
8	11.31 New frame 4.37	72	3	1944 Underframe to	11.75
9	11.31 New frame 2.37	74		DS70208, 8.64	
4410	5.32	3.63	4	1944	6.61
1	5.32	6.61	5	1944 Underframe to	2.67
2	6.32	11.64		DS70046, 11.59	
3	6.32	6.61	6	1944	6.61
4	6.32 *	6.61	7	1944 Underframe to	2.67
5	6.32 *	6.61		DS70047, 11.59	
6	8.32 *	6.61	8	1944 Underframe to	2.67
7	8.32 *	6.61		DS70048, 11.59	
8	8.32 *	6.61	9	1944 Underframe to	2.67
9	10.32	76		DS70049, 11.59	
4420	10.32	76	4450	1944	6.61
1	10.32	c.77	1	1944	c.73
2	10.32	c.77	2	1943	9.55
3	10.32	c75	3	1944	7.65
4	10.32 To ADS4424	?	4	1944 Underframe to	6.74
5	2.33 *	6.61		DS70209, 8.64	
6	2.33 *	6.61	5	1943	c.78
7	5.33	74	6	1943 To DS4456	?
8	5.33	73	7	1943	76
9	9.33	76	8	1944	76
4430	9.33	80	9	1944 To DS4459	c.86
1	9.33	c.78	4460	1944	c.78
2	9.33	c.78	1	1944	74
3	4.35 To TDB975452,	c.89	2	1944	c.78
	74		3	1944	c.78
4	4.35 To TDS4434,	?	4	1944	76
	74		5	1944	76
5	12.37	c.78	4466	1944	c.78

Notes

Nos. 4404–9/19–24/27–37/39–42/51/55–66 were transferred to freight stock 2.1970.

DS70046–9 were water tanks, to work between New Basford and Annesley.

DS70208/9 were crane equipment wagons at Stewarts Lane and Feltham motive power depots respectively.

* Mobile tank carrier wagons.

Bogie scenery vans Nos. 4581 and 4583 at Southampton Terminus. The bodies were built at Eastleigh in December 1928 on the underframes of ex-LB & SC composites of 1901, refitted with ex-LSW bogies. Note the end-loading doors and high roof of steel plates. *F. Foote*

Scenery van No. 4590, built at Ashford (*underframe*) and Eastleigh (*body*) in October 1938, newly repainted green in April 1949. *A.E. West*

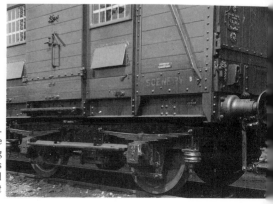

Bogie and bodyside details of scenery van No. 4590. On the solebar is visible the paint date '41 – 29.4.49', 41 being the code for Lancing Works. Note also on the end three plates giving the tare, overall length and width, and route restriction. *A.E. West*

Chapter Ten

Bogie Scenery Vans

There were 30 of these highly distinctive vans built in three batches of 10 at approximately 10-year intervals. They were about 50 ft long over body, but the special feature was the very high arched, steel roof, making the vehicles 12 ft 8 in. from rail to top of roof – 4 inches higher than a Maunsell coach. The vans, which also had end-loading doors of the same design as those on utility vans, were intended for carriage of large items such as theatrical scenery, circus equipment – and even elephants. They would have run in special trains and were not usually found in ordinary van trains.

The first 10 were authorised in April 1925 but were not built until late 1928/early 1929. Although the bodies (built at Eastleigh) were new, the underframes were not. Ten former London, Brighton & South Coast Railway bogie coaches, built by the Birmingham Railway Carriage & Wagon Co. in 1901, had their bodies re-used in electric train stock in 1928 and the leftover underframes found their way under the scenery vans, which received the numbers 4577–86 (Diagram No. 3181). London & South Western bogies were used to replace the LBSC bogies.

Tare weight was 24 tons and each van could load up to 10 tons. No. 4584 was specially equipped for tethering elephants, but how many at a time does not seem to have been recorded.

In 1930, 10 more scenery trucks were authorised for completion in 1931 but they were not built, presumably because of shortage of money. The order was deferred in 1933, but in March 1937 the 10 vans were again authorised and this time they were built. They even had new underframes – built at Ashford – and the bodies came out of Eastleigh, being completed in October and November 1938 to Order No. A975. Because the underframes were different from those of the early batch (bogie centres were 34 ft 10 in. as opposed to 33 ft) they had a different diagram number – 3182. Vehicle numbers were 4587–96.

The final batch of 10 was built, perhaps surprisingly, after nationalisation. Lancing Works constructed Nos. 4597–4606 in 1949 to Order No. L3228. They were virtually identical to the 1938 batch, the chief differences being that some of them had no rain strips over the bodyside doors and the roofs had 14 strengthening ribs, whereas the 1938 vans had only 10. Nos. 4597–4606 weighed 25 tons.

Nos. 4577–86, with their now ancient underframes, were withdrawn between 1959 and 1961 and all were scrapped, including the 'elephant van'. Three of the remaining 20 vans, Nos. 4589, 4598 and 4601, were equipped for tethering elephants, more than making up the shortfall.

A fairly regular destination for the vans was Victoria, where scenery for the London theatres was unloaded at the buffers of the centre road between Platforms 16 and 17.

Even when the traffic for which the vans had been designed trickled away, and circus and theatrical trains had been consigned to history, the vans, classified GUV by BR, continued in use; they were merely employed indiscriminately as parcels vans and formed in parcels trains as required.

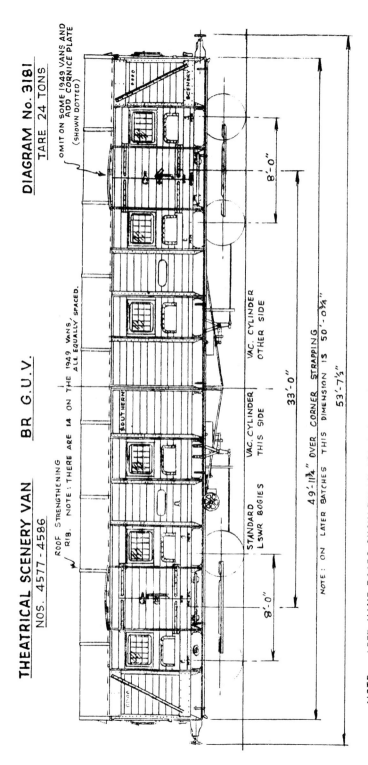

THEATRICAL SCENERY VAN   BR G.U.V.

NOS. 4577 - 4586

DIAGRAM No. 3181

TARE 24 TONS

OMIT ON SOME 1949 VANS AND ADD CORNICE PLATE
(SHOWN DOTTED)

ROOF STRENGTHENING
RIB. NOTE: THERE ARE 14 ON THE 1949 VANS,
ALL EQUALLY SPACED.

SCENERY

SOUTHERN

VAC. CYLINDER
OTHER SIDE

VAC. CYLINDER
THIS SIDE

STANDARD
LSWR BOGIES

8'-0"

8'-0"

33'-0"

49'-11¾" OVER CORNER STRAPPING

NOTE: ON LATER BATCHES THIS DIMENSION IS 50'-0¾"

53'-7½"

DRAWN BY
M. S. KING

NOTE: LEFT-HAND DOORS SHOW DETAIL FOR 1928-BUILT VANS.
RIGHT-HAND DOORS APPLY TO 1938 AND 1949 BATCHES.

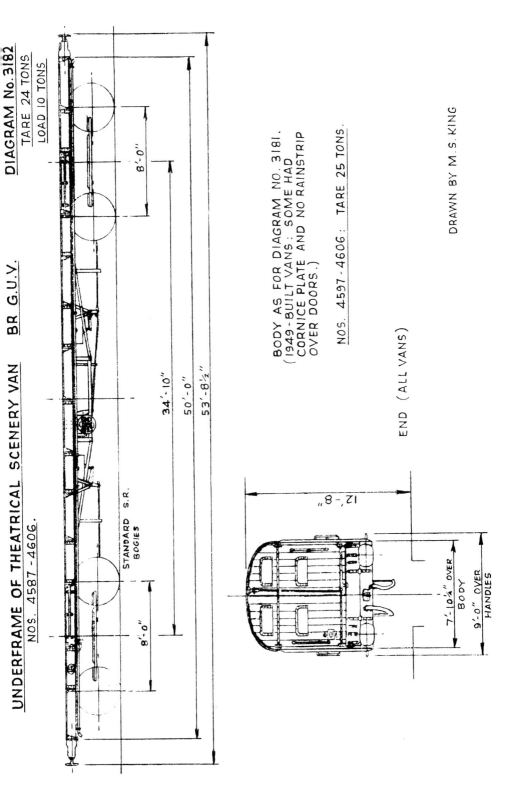

UNDERFRAME OF THEATRICAL SCENERY VAN   BR G.U.V.   DIAGRAM No. 3182

NOS. 4587 - 4606.

TARE 24 TONS
LOAD 10 TONS

STANDARD S.R. BOGIES

8'-0"

8'-0"

34'-10"

50'-0"

53'-8½"

BODY AS FOR DIAGRAM NO. 3181.
(1949-BUILT VANS: SOME HAD
CORNICE PLATE AND NO RAINSTRIP
OVER DOORS.)

NOS. 4597-4606:   TARE 25 TONS.

END (ALL VANS)

12'-8"

7'-10½" OVER BODY

9'-0" OVER HANDLES

DRAWN BY M. S. KING

The green livery hidden by dirt gave way to blue hidden by dirt. On 6th August, 1969 No. S4602S in blue livery turned up at Cambridge in a Parcels Express train formed mainly of BR general utility vans. On 5th June, 1975 No. S4605 was included in the formation of the 2.45 am Waterloo to Bournemouth; owing to the derailment of a preceding train, the 2.45 never got to Bournemouth that morning but terminated at Eastleigh after running via Guildford and Fareham!

Gradual withdrawal of the vans was made during the 1970s, the last going in 1979 and 1980. However, quite a few were subsequently converted for departmental use, the most noteworthy being the two altered in 1980 for Chipman's weedkilling train. Nos. 4604/5 became TDB 975966/7 and were used as stores vans for this train. Two vans have been preserved: No. 4594 of 1938 by the Swanage Railway in 1977; and No. 4601 of 1949 by the Bluebell Railway in August 1981. It was in fact the last example in capital stock on BR.

BOGIE SCENERY VANS
Summary of Building and Withdrawal Dates

	Built	Underframe ex	Built	Withdrawn	Remarks
4577	11.28	LBSC1563 Third	1901	9.59	
8	12.28	LBSC574 Compo	1901	11.59	
9	12.28	LBSC575 Compo	1901	by 9.61	
4580	12.28	LBSC1572 Third	1901	by 6.64	
1	12.28	LBSC571 Compo	1901	2.62	
2	12.28	LBSC570 Compo	1901	2.59	
3	12.28	SR6088 Compo	1901	9.60	
4	12.28	SR6089 Compo	1901	9.59	
5	1.29	LBSC572 Compo	1901	5.60	
6	1.29	LBSC573 Compo	1901	11.60	
7	11.38			c.6.76	
8	11.38				To 083361, 5.79
9	11.38			?	To CC99015
4590	10.38				To 083372, 9.79. Wdn c.89
1	10.38			c.2.79	
2	10.38			9.67	
3	10.38			c.4.77	To DB975663, 1978
4	10.38			c.77	
5	11.38			c.78	
6	11.38			c.8.78	
7	1949				To ADB975890, 1979. Wdn c.89
8	1949				To 083379, 10.79
9	1949				To TDB975894, 1979. Wdn c.89
4600	1949			c.4.80	To CC99014
1	1949			80	
2	1949				To ADB975889, 1979. Wdn c.89
3	1949	Burnt out at Newington 31.8.75			
4	1949				To TDB975966, 1980
5	1949				To TDB975967, 1980
4606	1949				To 060957, 2.81

Scenery van No. 4596, built at Ashford and Eastleigh in November 1938.
M.S. King Collection

Chipman weedkilling train at Newhaven Harbour station, with stores van No. TDB 975966, altered in 1980 from scenery van No. 4604, one of ten built at Lancing in 1949. Picture taken on 24th April, 1982. *Author*

Post office sorting van No. 4919, built in December 1936. It had no lavatory, unlike the later examples, such as the van coupled next to No. 4919. Weymouth, 7th September, 1963. *P.H. Swift*

Post office sorting van No. 4922, corridor side, built at Eastleigh in 1939. Posting box at left-hand end, two sliding doors, and lavatory at right-end end.

Courtesy National Railway Museum

Post office tender, or stowage van, No. 4959, built at Lancing (*underframe*) and Eastleigh (*body*) in March 1939. Two sliding doors each side, off-centre gangway, but no accommodation for sorters.　　　　　　　　　　　*Courtesy HM.R.S.*

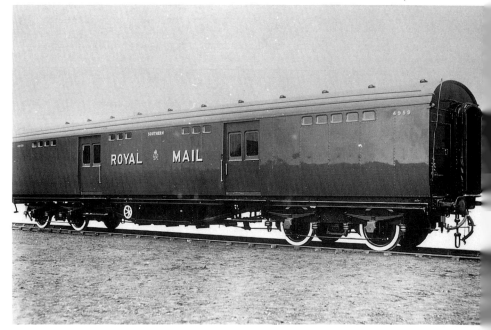

Chapter Eleven
Post Office Vans

At a Rolling Stock Committee meeting on 6th March, 1936, Maunsell reported that he had in hand the construction of a Post Office sorting van to replace one that no longer met Post Office requirements. He stated that the GPO was contributing about £575 towards its cost.

This was the first new sorting van built by the Southern; pre-Grouping mail vans had been and continued to be used for many years, the chief mail routes being Waterloo to Dorchester and London Bridge to Dover, which were served by postal trains to which a passenger coach or two were added. A mail sorting van also worked between Holborn Viaduct and Newhaven Harbour, being attached to the down evening boat train from Victoria at East Croydon and detached from the up early-morning train at the same place.

The new van, No. 4919, was completed to Order No. 879 and put into service in December 1936. It had a body length of 58 ft, width of 9 ft, and its height from rail to roof-top was 12 ft 4 in. There was one set of double doors on one side and two sliding doors on the other. To conform to standard practice for mail vans at that time off-centre gangways were fitted at both ends, but there was no lavatory compartment – a surprising omission. The diagram number was 3191.

In 1939 there appeared three more sorting vans and, to go with them, four stowage vans. The sorting vans, built at Eastleigh to Order No. 1043, Diagram No. 3192, were numbered 4920–2; they had the same dimensions and general layout as No. 4919 but each was equipped additionally with a lavatory compartment and adjacent sink. The stowage vans, whose underframes were built at Lancing and bodies at Eastleigh to Order No. 999 (Diagram 3196), were numbered 4957–60. They had the same overall dimensions as the sorting vans and, like them, were fitted with off-centre gangways. Otherwise they were just empty shells, without sorting pigeon-holes; access was by two sliding doors on each bodyside and illumination was given by small toplights.

Each of the sorting cars had a letter-box which the public could use for late posting, and letters posted there had to bear an extra stamp.

All the new vans except No. 4957 were allocated to the Western Section and worked in the same link as ex-London & South Western vans. Three sorting cars and two stowage vans were required in traffic, plus one of each standing spare. Services worked were the 10.30 pm Waterloo to Dorchester via Southampton Terminus (2 sorting, 1 stowage) and 9.55 pm Dorchester to Waterloo via Southampton Terminus (2 sorting, 1 stowage).

Stowage van No. 4957 went to the Eastern Section to work in the same link as ex-South Eastern & Chatham vans on the London Bridge–Dover mail trains. These ran via Redhill, the old main-line route, in both directions. The down service left London Bridge about 11.50 pm; the up left Dover Marine at 10.40 pm and conveyed a coach for third class passengers. During the War this service was suspended and in 1941 No. 4957 was stored at Epsom Downs station, along with eight ex-SEC Post Office vans.

Working of sorting cars was suspended also on the Western Section for the duration of the War, but the stowage vans remained in use on the Dorchester service. By March 1941 the 10.30 pm departure from Waterloo had been altered to start from Surbiton at 10.45 pm; presumably this was to avoid the worst of the nightly bombing of London at that time. By 1944 the train had resumed its Waterloo departure. During the War, stowage vans Nos. 4959 and 4960 were diagrammed, one on the down and one on the up service; No. 4958 stood spare as relief.

In November 1943 sorting vans Nos. 4920/2 and stowage van No. 4957 were temporarily renumbered 1888S, 1882S and 1884S in the Service Vehicles list and used for the storage of Air Raid Precautions equipment and clothing at Strood, Windsor and Lewes respectively. One ex-LSW and four ex-SEC PO vans were also used for the same purpose, each being berthed at a different location.

All the PO vans were returned to traffic in 1946, as were the remaining pre-Grouping vehicles. Formation of both the 10.30 pm Waterloo to Dorchester and the 10.20 pm Dorchester to Waterloo was 2 sorting cars, 1 stowage van, and several vans plus passenger accommodation. Van No. 4957 returned to the Eastern Section, working with ex-SEC Post Office vans in the 11.50 pm London Bridge to Dover and 10.40 pm Dover to Cannon Street both of which now conveyed a corridor third class coach for passengers.

Allocations of the vans from 1948 onwards were as shown below:

> 4919 Waterloo–Dorchester, 1948–57; Spare, 1957–60; Waterloo–Dorchester, 1960–66.
> 4920 Waterloo–Dorchester, 1948–57; Spare, 1957–60; Waterloo–Dorchester, 1960–66.
> 4921 Waterloo–Dorchester, 1948–66.
> 4922 Spare, 1948–57; Waterloo–Dorchester, 1957–66.
> 4957 London Bridge–Dover, 1948–60; Spare as relief to 4959 and 4960, 1960–62.
> 4958 Spare, 1948–66.
> 4959 Waterloo–Dorchester, 1948–66.
> 4960 Waterloo–Dorchester, 1948–66.

There were also two ex-LSW PO Vans operating in the Dorchester service, though it seems strange that from 1957 to 1960 the more modern SR vehicles (Nos. 4919/20) were kept spare as relief to these.

In 1960 the Dover service began to be operated with a batch of ex-Great Western PO vans fitted with electric heating (Nos. 806–8 and 812–4) and this caused the transfer of No. 4957 to the South Western Division. However, it was not really required there and two years later was packed off to the London Midland Region, disappearing from Southern Region lists. Two more ex-GW sorting cars, No. 846/7, went to the South Western Division in 1960 as relief to the Southern vehicles.

Times of the down and up Dorchester mail trains in 1960 were 10.35 pm and 10.38 pm respectively, and each train still included two sorting cars and one stowage van. In 1966 the vans were arranged to run to and from Weymouth, presumably because of withdrawal of TPO facilities from Paddington to Weymouth, and this practice continued for several years. Nos. 4919–22 and 4958–60 continued to be used on the Waterloo–

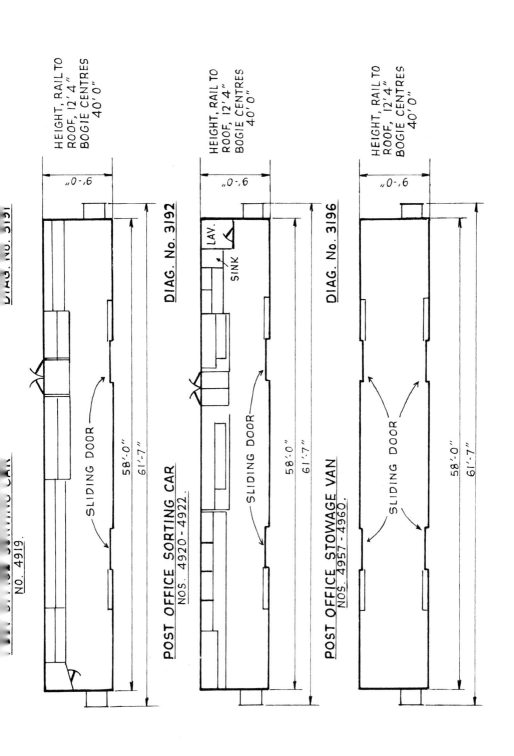

DIAG. No. 3191

NO. 4919.

HEIGHT, RAIL TO
ROOF, 12' 4"
BOGIE CENTRES
40' 0"

9'-0"

58'-0"

61'-7"

SLIDING DOOR

DIAG. No. 3192

POST OFFICE SORTING CAR
NOS. 4920 - 4922.

HEIGHT, RAIL TO
ROOF, 12' 4"
BOGIE CENTRES
40' 0"

9'-0"

LAV.

SINK

58'-0"

61'-7"

SLIDING DOOR

DIAG. No. 3196

POST OFFICE STOWAGE VAN
NOS. 4957 - 4960.

HEIGHT, RAIL TO
ROOF, 12' 4"
BOGIE CENTRES
40' 0"

9'-0"

58'-0"

61'-7"

SLIDING DOOR

Weymouth service from 1966 until about 1973. With the end of steam locomotive operation in July 1967 it was necessary to equip the vans with electric heaters, and this work was carried out in 1966/7; they were also repainted in blue and grey, the only SR-design vehicles to wear this livery.

About 1973 No. 4919, the solitary sorting van without lavatory, was withdrawn and, after modern BR Post Office vans had arrived in 1973 to take over the working of the Weymouth postal, the six Southern survivors were transferred in 1974 to the South Eastern Division to work the Dover mail trains, in replacement of four ex-LMS vehicles that had themselves replaced the ex-GW PO vans about 1970/1.

The Dover service had been revised in 1971 so that instead of there being two trains, each making its single nightly journey, there was now only one train doing the return trip each day, Sundays to Fridays. One sorting car was therefore in traffic with two 'spare and maintenance'; and one stowage van was in traffic with two 'spare and maintenance'. The workings in 1974, 1975 and 1976 were at 6.55 pm from Dover Priory to Victoria and 11.54 pm return; there was no passenger accommodation.

However, late in 1976, the Dover mail trains ceased altogether and by March 1977 the six cars were collected together in Selhurst scrap sidings; all were condemned in March 1977 after an active life of nearly 38 years. Three were preserved: No. 4920 went to the railway museum at York, No. 4922 to the Bluebell Railway in March 1978, and No. 4958 to the Mid-Hants Railway in September 1977. The other three were sold for scrap to Kings of Snailwell in December 1977.

Sorting van No. 4920, in BR blue and grey livery, at Ashford on 5th June, 1975. It was built at Eastleigh in June 1939 for the Waterloo–Dorchester service and transferred to the Dover mail service in 1974. Note the electric heating connections below the buffers.   *Author*

Appendix

4 mm Scale Models of SR Passenger Vans

It may be of interest to modelmakers to know just what has been available to the Southern enthusiast for his layout since the 1950s. A great many kits for SR coaches, vans and wagons were produced by just two firms, CCW and Ratio, between 1951 and 1955; but after that there was almost nothing in the rolling stock line and in the 1960s manufacturers concentrated on locomotive kits. It was a very curious situation.

The Webster Development Company – otherwise known as Ratio – was the first to produce van kits for the Southern modeller. The bogie luggage van and the 4-wheel utility van were both introduced in October 1954; both were wooden body kits only, and the purchaser was expected to make up his own bogies and to obtain the necessary wheels and couplings. The kits, in 1 mm birch ply, were highly accurate and beautifully finished, with the planking ready scribed. Both were available for only a short time, as in 1958 Ratio stopped making wooden kits and changed over to plastic. The vans were never re-introduced in the new material, but in 1986 Ratio brought out a Van B in plastic. This was a magnificent kit, with fully detailed parts (some being etched brass) and, unlike the 1954 kits, was absolutely complete. The door planking was not quite correctly represented, but otherwise it was a well-nigh perfect model.

Ratio's great rival in the field of wooden coach kits was CCW Productions (Cramer, Cartwright, Webster). This company began in 1950 by producing timber parts to make up coaches to the modeller's own requirement; later, coach body kits were sold. The original proprietor, H.G. Cramer, sold the business to A.F. Inglefield in 1952, and his erstwhile partner, Jack Webster, founded Ratio. No sooner had Ratio produced their Southern vans than CCW were advertising, in January 1955, kits of precisely the same vehicles, the corridor luggage van and the 4-wheel utility van. They were among the first of CCW's complete kits; up till then CCW too had made separate body and underframe kits, the wheels and couplings for which had to be purchased separately. CCW's corridor luggage van was not such a good model as Ratio's; the scribed planking was wrong and the windows were a little too high up the bodyside. The wooden kits in 4 mm scale began to be run down in 1959 and were discontinued in 1962 when the company decided to concentrate solely on 7 mm.

K's (N. & K. Keyser) produced a very good white-metal utility van kit, which was first advertised in June 1957. 'All super detail cast parts – wheels and couplings extra,' said their advertisement in the *Model Railway News*. There was no floor, either, or glazing; in later years wheels were provided. The kit, which represented one of the earliest batch of the Van U, was easy to assemble; so easy that it was considered unnecessary to include any instructions! It was available for many years but, in the 1970s, it was replaced by a plastic kit that was nowhere near as good, since the planking was given a curious half-round profile which was quite wrong.

In March 1958 Tri-ang (Rovex Scale Models) produced a bogie luggage van – the first item of Southern stock they had made. The plastic body was quite a fair representation, and all twelve doors could be opened, the pivot-ends of the T-hinges forming stops at just over 90 degrees and snap-locks if the doors were pushed back against the van sides. There were several inaccuracies, mainly due to the fact that standard Tri-ang components were used, and the body was slightly *longer* than scale. The roof profile was incorrect, as were the underframe and bogies, which were the same as those used on Tri-ang's shortened version of the BR MkI coach. Despite this, the *Model Railway News* averred that 'detail under the solebars gives the model a very nice profile.' Never mind that it was utterly wrong for the SR! The *Railway Modeller* gushed over 'this superb-detail wagon', but not all the detail was correct; in particular, liberties had to be taken with the doors in order that they could be made to open. The van was available in BR red or green, with the number S2357S (that of a 53 ft 3 in. van). The overall effect was good, and the model was much better than most of Tri-ang's others at the time. The *MRN* stated that 'cross strapping at either end fails to join verticals' – but it wasn't supposed to!

In December 1961 yet another 4-wheel utility van was put on the market, this time by Hornby-Dublo. It was a very accurate model in plastic of one of the 1938 batch, with wide-and-narrow body planking but equally-planked doors. 'The moulded detail on the body is truly amazing, and the opening doors are commendably neat,' drooled the *Railway Modeller* in January 1962. It was a pity that the doors *were* made to open for, as with the Tri-ang vehicle, some liberties were taken that did spoil the appearance slightly. The given number, S2380S, was wrong for this particular model; correct numbers would have been 1731–80. Colour was bright green, lighter than the correct BR coach green.

Hornby-Dublo introduced a United Dairies 6-wheel milk tank wagon in August 1962. It was similar in appearance to the SR's 4404–9 batch (Diagram No. 3159), with centrally-placed ladder and six cradles to support the tank. The letters 'U D' appeared large on the tank. The model is thought to have been based on a GW design.

In recent years Parkside Dundas have produced some very good plastic kits of passenger vans. The PMV could be assembled as either the SEC or SR version, and by 1990 the 4-wheel brake van was available. In September 1990 the CCT was introduced. With these and Ratio's Van B the Southern modeller is better provided with passenger van kits than he has been for many years, though it is sad that the pioneering timber body kits of the 1950s had such a short run.

Cover: 4-wheel guard's van No. 653, built at Ashford in September 1938. This view, taken at Horsted Keynes on 7th April, 1991, shows a pair of doors giving access to one of the luggage compartments. The arrangement of the planking and strapping is well shown in this view. *D. Gould*

Cover: Part of the body of SE&C luggage van No. 153 – which became Southern No. 1994 in 1930 and DS70031 in 1959 – at Horsted Keynes on 7th April, 1991. SR-built vans had a bodyside ventilator under each window, but the SE&C vans did not. *D. Gould*